Disgusting Diseases
A YOUNG PERSON'S GUIDE

Disgusting Diseases

A YOUNG PERSON'S GUIDE

Pandora's Box – the world's ills are unleashed upon humanity.

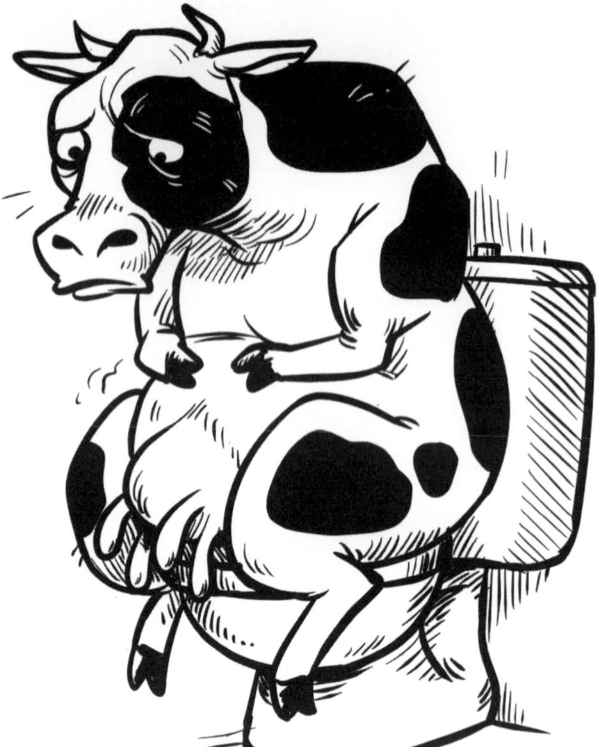

Contents

Introduction 9

CHAPTER 1 – *Dirt* 17

CHAPTER 2 – *Ebola* 33

CHAPTER 3 – *Parasites, Worms & Bugs* 41

CHAPTER 4 – *Rabies* 57

CHAPTER 5 – *Miscellaneous Maladies* 65

CHAPTER 6 – *Typhoid And Typhus* 77

CHAPTER 7 – *Crazy Cures* 89

CHAPTER 8 – *The Black Death* 107

CHAPTER 9 – *Bloodsuckers And Malaria* .. 123

CHAPTER 10 – *Death* 139

Glossary of terms 151

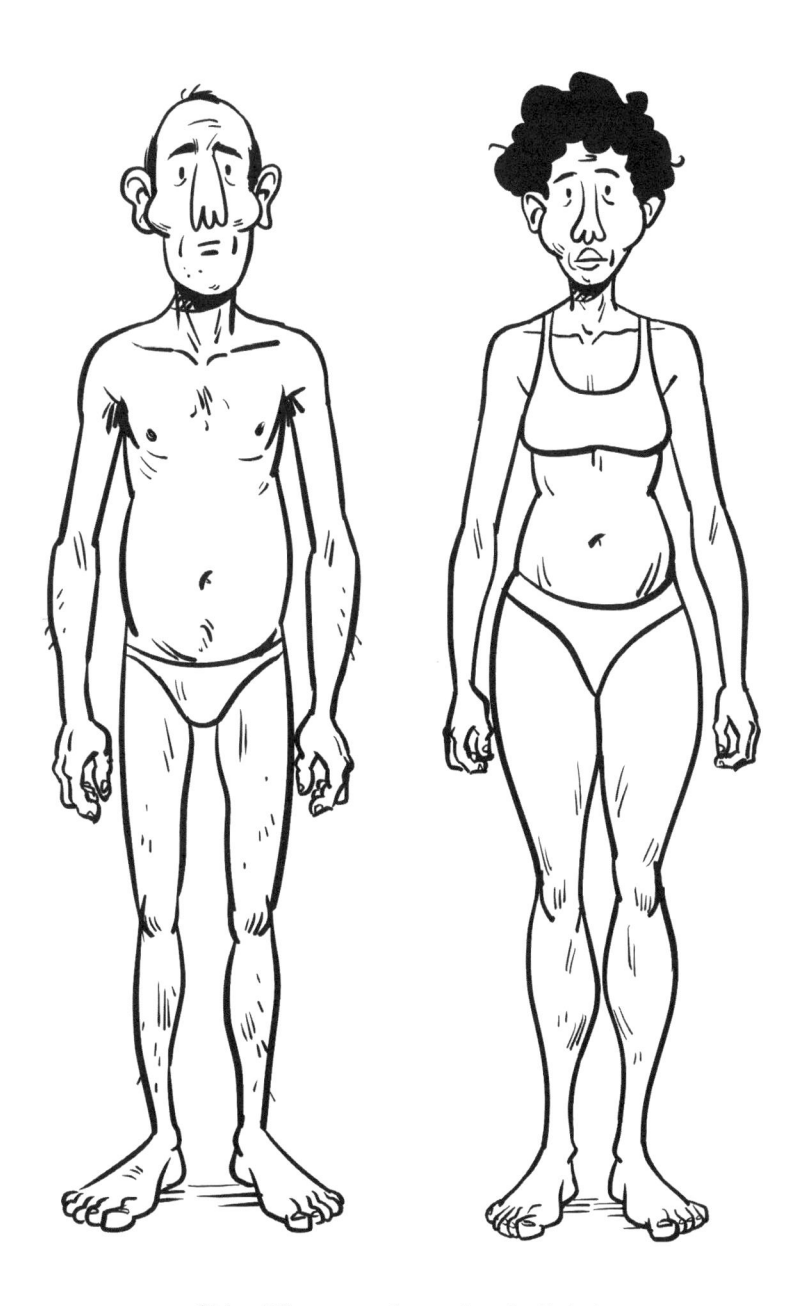

Rick and Rita – your unfortunate hosts for this book.

INTRODUCTION

PAM can kill. I don't mean the nice girl, Pamela Winterbottom, in Year Seven; I mean P.A.M. which stands for Primary Amebic Meningoencephalitis, which in English means 'the disease that happens when a bug gets in your brain and eats it.'

The bug in question is a little 'amoeba' that is found in warm water in many places, including the southern states of the USA.

N. FOWLERI

Naegleria fowleri is a creepy little single cell animal that loves to breed in warm water, and the warmer the better. Creepy doesn't mean slightly scary it actually means that the amoeba gets up people's noses when they are having a nice swim, goes up the nasal canal (the passage behind your nose that stings if you get fizzy drink up there), and creeps straight into the brain!

Inside the head of a human is a perfect place for N. fowleri, once there it begins to breed. It snacks on your brain and turns it into millions and billions of new amoebae.

"Mmmmmmm. Brains." Once Naegleria fowleri gets stuck in there's no escape.

If you are unlucky enough to get this disease you won't know about it for about one or two weeks. Then, all of a sudden, you'll get a bit of a headache followed by nausea and a stiff neck. As the disease progresses confusion and hallucinations follow. After 5 days you're dead. About 97% of people who get this disease die of it which is pretty grim. Fortunately, it is very very very rare and there have only been about 100 cases in recorded history.

Another disease which is almost as horrible is called necrotising fasciitis it's a nasty bacterium that is picked up in tropical places. The first symptom is like a little pimple like spot on your skin. Bacteria are single cell organisms just a few micrometers (means pretty darn small) in length. This is the hole where the bacteria enter your flesh and then they begin to eat away at your muscles, tendons and bones. On the outside your skin might look fine, but this bug is turning your flesh into 'necrotic' (dead) tissue which is, of course, where the name for this comes from. Fasciitis is Latin for 'swollen flesh' so the full name is 'dead swollen flesh disease'. Considering it can eat away your arm, your leg, your bum or even your face (don't search this disease in images google – I warn you) this is one pretty unpleasant little bug. Thankfully if it's caught quick enough the chances of survival are pretty good. Antibiotics and quick 'surgical intervention' (cutting off dead flesh) can usually limit the damage.

But, you may ask, how can a tiny little organism cause such mayhem and madness on a poor person's body. The first time early humans (hominids) stood upright was about 4 million years ago – Homo sapien sapien (clever upright man) probably emerged from Africa about 70,000 years ago. That seems an awfully long time that we've been wandering the globe, but it is believed that the first bacteria emerged **FOUR BILLION YEARS** ago. For **THREE BILLION YEARS** they were the dominant lifeform on earth and spread into soil, acidic hot springs, deep into the earth's crust and even into the lowest part of the ocean. They have been found 11 kilometers down in the Marianas Trench. Today they can live in radiation affected nuclear waste dumps and there is evidence that bacteria are still thriving on Mars

"We're all going on a radiation holiday." Bacteria can thrive in any environment.

About 700 million years ago multicellular life evolved and the bacteria leapt at the chance to eat, live on and breed on new hosts. Even now Bacteria are your BFF. In your gut about 1,000 different species of bacteria thrive, breaking down your food. They are also all over your skin, on your eyes, in your nose and everywhere else that I don't want to talk about. Most of these bacteria are harmless, even good for you, but when a crazy brave bacterium like necrotising fasciitis gets where it shouldn't, four billion years of evolutionary history kick in and you're history! This book will tell you about a lot of other nasty bacteria that can play merry havoc with our frail bodies.

But, Bacteria aren't the only nasty single cell critters around. There's another critter called a 'protozoa', which are a type of parasite. Parasites are the next nasty way that humans can be attacked by members of the natural world. Protozoa is perhaps the smallest parasite, similar in size to bacteria, but they are much more sophisticated and can move around and feed just like animals.

A particularly nasty one recently hit the world headlines when a group of explorers discovered the City of the Monkey God deep in rainforest on the border of Nicaragua and Honduras.

Watch out for the curse of the Monkey God – one of the smallest killers of all.

The explorers had a great deal of difficulty cutting their way through the dense jungle and fighting off poisonous snakes. After months of hacking their way through the jungle they came upon a series of huge temples covered by towering trees and vines. It soon became obvious that no one had been there since it had been abandoned more than 500 years ago. The population of this once mighty metropolis, which was founded about 1000 CE, had fled all those centuries ago. They left behind countless valuable artefacts because they thought the whole site had been cursed by disease.

This curse was no fable, once the explorers broke through the jungle onto the stone ruins a cloud of voracious sandflies descended on them. The sandflies bit through their clothes and left itchy, raised wounds. The sandflies weren't only taking blood. They left the horrible parasite Leishmaniosis which is like a tiny wriggly worm that creates horrible looking sores as it eats away at, you guessed it, your skin (there's also another form that eats away your internal organs and even your bone marrow). These sores are called 'lesions' and can be all in one spot or scattered all over the body, wherever the poor victim got bitten. This disease is all around the world and has lots of names; Kala Azar, Dum Dum Fever, Black Fever and Sandfly Disease. These have been found in fossil records in the Cretaceous, so they've been feasting on animals for at least 145 million years.

In this book you'll read a lot about different parasites that have decided to take up residence on and in us poor old homo sapiens, living in our guts, nesting in our brain or settling under the skin.

Which takes us to our last major type of nasty that launches attacks on our frail vessels – viruses. Viruses are the smallest known life form on earth, (except perhaps for the yeast – but don't get me started on yeasts, they have no known earthlike DNA and could in fact be from outer space –just like the prions, but don't get me started on the prions) they don't even comprise a single cell. They are small strands of DNA like material and can't survive for a long time without a host cell to infect. They may be small but they are not to be underestimated. There are about 320,000 known viruses and about 200 of these are able to target your body and wreak merry havoc. They can enter your body through food, air, fluids or animal bites. Once they are inside you, they turn you into a virus factory, replicating the little nasties and spreading them to your loved ones and even your enemies.

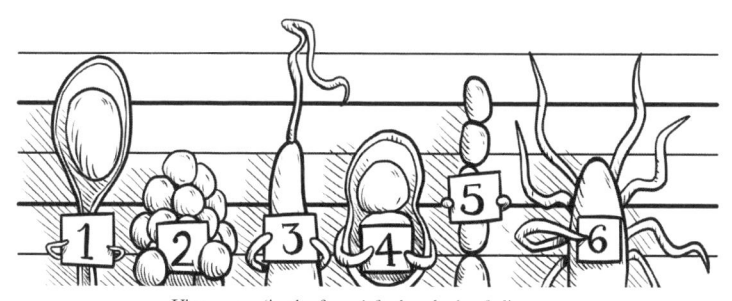

Viruses are 'in the frame' for hundreds of diseases.

The best-known virus, and the one you are likely to come in contact with, is the 'influenza' virus. Influenza causes its victims to cough, splutter, sneeze and snot. Millions of flu viruses are in each tiny globule of snot and if you are unfortunate enough to touch one of these or breathe it in – you're snotted too.

The common cold is a fairly harmless virus (it can be good if you wangle a day or two off school) but others are lethal with a capital 'L'. Ebola definitely comes into this grade as it can kill in a matter of days and liquefy a poor person's innards. Another virus in the lethal category is HIV, a sexually transmitted disease but we probably won't talk too much about how to get it because this is, after all, *Disgusting Diseases – A **Young** Person's Guide.*

Bugs are in a continuous state of germ warfare and are always trying to outwit us humans to take advantage of us. Just as you want to live as long as possible (and even longer), so do germs. That means that bacteria and viruses have developed thousands of ways of surviving, using us as their tools. Some try to overwhelm our defenses and make us mucus/blood machines that infect anybody who comes close. Others hide away in our system waiting to spring out so that they can infect us or people we come into contact with. These are '**GERM SURVIVAL STRATEGIES**'.

In these books we'll look at other ways you can get sick such as different cancers (voted number one the scariest word in the English language, probably seconded by 'homework') and also ways that we can be cured. Most diseases now have cures and medical technology has gone gangbusters in the last two hundred years so you and I are really really lucky to be living right now.

You people are darn lucky – out of all of the past generations you have the longest life expectancy ever. Soon women will be living until they are 120 and men until they are 115. You never know – maybe stem cell therapy will allow people to live for hundreds of years.

There are even moves afoot to make us immortal by downloading your consciousness into machines. I'm not sure about that – surely you wouldn't be you once the brains contents cross that flesh/electricity divide. But who knows.

FANTASTIC FACTS
THE AQUATIC APE THEORY

If you do die earlier, it will probably be from heart disease, which is the scourge of modern world. This is caused when fats build up in the body – placing pressure on the heart. When fats and other things build up in the arteries blood flow is restricted and this leads to heart attacks.

The reason we have so much fat might be because we were possibly swimming apes. Humans are different from all of our primate relatives because we have large fatty deposits under the skin of our faces, buttocks, chest and limbs, whereas our cousins – chimpanzees, gorillas and orangutans – have the wrinkly flesh characteristic of all other primates and lack subcutaneous (under the skin) fat deposits.

The 'aquatic ape' theory says that millions of years ago our hairy, skinny, four legged ancestors went into the water of some lakes in Africa and came out bipedal, with subcutaneous fat and without any hair, except on our heads. During that time our spine straightened out to make it easier to swim, we got extra fat, as it helps us float and keep warm, and we had hair on our head so the little baby apes could hold on while we paddled around.

You might think this is a bit of a silly theory but just think; all mammals that swim, such as dugongs, whales, and dolphins are hairless, have straight spines and have lots of blubber. Hippos are similar.

It is possible that we may have been in the lakes for one million years or so, evolving an upright posture. Then, when the lakes dried out, we emerged fully fledged upright hominids.

Next time you see a picture of an early hominid like an Australopithecus or a Homo erectus ask your self did the artist get it wrong – should they all look hairless with fatty faces just like us?

BAD MANNERS IN THE MIDDLE AGES
– 'Greetings sir, how goes your poo?'

CHAPTER 1

Dirt

Diseases' best friend

"It is impolite to greet someone who is urinating or defecating." So said the wise man Erasmus. Erasmus lived in the Middle Ages when it was common that if you needed to do 'Ones and Twos' (# See glossary) you'd drop your pants wherever you wanted and do your business. Erasmus was obviously a polite fellow and didn't think it was good manners to shake a person's hands and strike up a conversation if they were 'otherwise engaged'.

This chapter deals with lots of smelly and horrible things and is pretty inappropriate for young people, but what the heck, I'm going to write it anyway. People used to be surrounded by the rotting smells of dead animals, urine, human waste and lots of other yucky things. Some religions say it was bad to wash and even kings would only change their trousers once a year! Instead of having flushing toilets people had large smelly cess-pits dug into the ground. Flies and rats loved getting in there, having a good feed, and spreading around all manner of shocking smelly bugs.

Before modern medicine people didn't know that it was really important to wash your hands. Bacteria and a whole lot of nasty germs love waiting under people's fingernails and jumping out to infect food and make people sick. Not only bacteria but also worm eggs, which most people used to be infected with, can live under fingernails for days.

But, believe it or not, early humans who were hunter-gatherers didn't have this problem and were really pretty healthy.

The Christian Bible tells the story that Adam and Eve lived in the Garden of Eden surrounded by all good things, had limitless amounts of food and never got sick. The they were kicked out of the Garden when they ate an apple offered by The Devil. Once out of the garden they could get sick and found life a lot tougher.

"We only had to follow one rule!" – Adam and Eve kicked out of the Garden of Eden.

Greek people had a myth about Pandora's Box. Pandora was a beautiful young lady and when she got married Zeus gave her a box filled with all a whole lot of nasties. Spiders, flies, sickness, disease and death were all contained in this box. Zeus told Pandora not to open the box, but of course her curiosity made her open it. All those nasty crawling critters escaped to make mankind's life a misery.

These stories might seem pretty funny to us but there is a little nugget of truth buried in each of them.

Bad move – Pandora lets out the world's ills.

When humans were hunter-gatherers they were very healthy and probably hadn't even heard of a lot of modern-day diseases. It was only when humans began to live in towns and farms that lots of modern day diseases crossed over. When we moved out of Eden, we were exposed to a whole lot of new ways to get very, very sick.

HUNTER-GATHERER EDEN

Early humans who lived during the Palaeolithic (old stone age) were hunter-gatherers. This led to an exceptionally healthy lifestyle where bands would roam the countryside sourcing food. Men would hunt and women would gather. One of the last groups of nomads to survive into the modern day were the Aboriginal Australians. As Captain Cook sailed up the east coast of Australia in 1770 he noted that compared to his scrawny English seamen the Aborigines were perfect specimens – tall, strong and without a care in the world.

When the first convicts arrived in Sydney harbour and founded Australia in 1788 they were extremely jealous of the aborigines. The natives would spend a couple of hours in the morning fishing in the harbour or digging yams. Once they had collected enough food they spent the rest of the day hanging out with each other, playing and laughing.

The nomadic lifestyle protected our ancestors. By constantly moving about they were able to leave their rubbish and excrement behind them. Germs, flies, worms and bugs thrive on this kind of stuff but the nomads would not usually be infected, they'd simply move on. One or two might get sick but not the whole tribe. They were very active and spent their day running, playing walking, climbing and fighting.

Hunter-gatherers were pretty healthy – and skinny.

If their water source wasn't crystal clear the inhabitants of the Palaeolithic could move on to fresh fields.

When a member of the tribe did become too weak to follow them on their migrations, because they were sick with a virus or some bacteria, the rest of the clan moved on leaving the sick individual behind. This may seem pretty heartless to us in the modern age who look after our old or sick family members, but it actually helped our ancestors survive. If a sick person stays with the tribe they can infect everybody else until one illness becomes and epidemic.

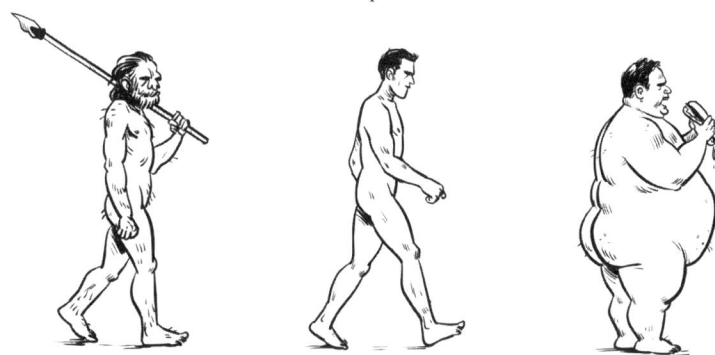

Homo heidelbergensis – Homo sapiens – Homo remotecontrolsis.

Early hunter-gatherer tribes sometimes lived in caves but it seems they had an idea about basic hygiene. Neanderthals lived in Europe from about 200,000 BCE to 30,000 BCE and often inhabited caves. Through this whole period their caves throughout their range have amazing similarities. At the front would be large hearth with tool making areas. At the rear of the cave, out of the way, was a charnel area where rubbish was disposed of. In the centre of the cave were the living and sleeping areas. It was not wise to dispose of bones out the front of the cave as they would attract predators, but at the back of the cave these bones and rubbish were well away from the living area to reduce contagious bugs. No coprolites (fossilised poo) has ever been found in these caves so they obviously went outside to do their business. Neanderthals often get some pretty bad press, but it seems that they were pretty darn hygienic, or at least as hygienic as you can get living outdoors all the time without showers, shampoo and dental floss. (Don't bag the Neanderthals – most modern humans have at least 3% Neanderthal DNA.)

But it wasn't all happy times and harmony in the Palaeolithic. Although the average age that they died at was 40 years old many received nasty knocks on the way. When you're an adult you may go out and wrestle with a 'thorny problem', a 'conundrum' or even a 'difficult workmate' but hunter-gatherers had to deal with dangerous animals such as woolly mammoths, cave lions, aurochs (very large, very angry cows), marsupial lions and a whole host of nasties and beasties. Many fossilised skeletons show signs of broken limbs, cracked heads and fractured ribs.

If there is one hero in ancient history it would have to be a Neanderthal nicknamed 'Nandy'. Found in the Shanidar cave in Iraq in 1957 Nandy had survived several broken legs, a broken hand, a broken foot and even a fractured skull above his left eye. All these wounds had healed, showing that Nandy was one tough character and that Palaeolithic folk had a pretty stupendous knowledge of healing broken bones.

'Nandy' was one tough character.

ANCIENT CANNIBALS

Big beasties with nasty clawsies and teethies were bad enough, but maybe the biggest threat to our stone age friends in the Palaeolithic were other hominids.

Many Homo habilis, Homo erectus and Homo heidelbergensis fossils have signs that they were chopped up after death with stone tools. Many, of course, were taken by animals and these bones show claw marks and bite marks. Those who were cooked up and eaten by near and dear relatives show cut marks. Also bones and brains were broken open so that all the juicy bits could be eaten! Other bones show traces of ancient fires so yes, you guessed it, some ancient humans were cooked before being eaten.

Evidence of cannibalism stretches way back into the past and could be considered 'normal' or everyday behaviour. 'Pioneer Man', Homo antecessor, butchered their dead family members at the same sites that they used to butcher animal carcasses 800,000 years ago.

Homo heidelbergensis living at Bodo in Ethiopia considered eyeballs a delicacy about 600,000 years ago. Cut marks on their skulls are mainly found around the eye sockets. One unfortunate 'Handy Man' Homo habilis had his jaw cut off by a stone tool 2 million years ago in Sterkfontein South Africa.

I'm not sure this is really relevant to a book that is meant to be about ancient diseases but it is a 'cracking yarn'.

FANTASTIC FACTS

BODY LICE HAVE BEEN WITH HUMANS FOR MILLIONS OF YEARS.

The DNA of gorilla lice and human lice began to change about 6 million years ago. So that's approximately how long ago our ancestors split from the other great apes.

Lice were also around when humans left Africa. We know this because as hunter-gatherers left Africa their skin color began to change as they moved into different environments. Today lice that live on Negroes have evolved to be black, if they live on Europeans they are white and if they live on Asians they are brown!

Eyeballs were a delicious delicacy for homo heidelbergensis!

NEOLITHIC FARMERS OPEN PANDORA'S BOX

Now, you've probably been told by some misguided teacher who doesn't really know what he or she is talking about that the invention of farming in the Neolithic (New Stone Age) was a really good thing. In fact, it has caused **UNTOLD MISERY** throughout the ages.

Once Neolithic people settled down to grow crops and raise animals so that they could feast on the new the foods, they also allowed other critters to feast on them! Many of these were tiny bugs and you'll read about them in other chapters. Humans never got Measles, Smallpox and Tuberculosis but once they began raising cows these diseases crossed into humanity. The clever farmers who learnt how to raise pigs and ducks probably didn't feel so smart when they caught the influenza virus. Some bright spark began raising chickens and allowed one of the biggest killers in the world into their family – Malaria.

The runs, Bali belly, the trots, flux, dysentery, Montezuma's revenge, gypy tummy, are all slang words for diarrhoea. There are a lot of other horrible descriptive terms for this pretty unpleasant condition but they are not really suitable for a book like this. Most people have encountered this nasty bug and you can blame our friends, domesticated cattle, for this one too. Norwalk virus jumped from cows to humans thousands of years ago and if you get a case of the trots it is probably because of this virus.

Next time you have a funny tummy – blame Bessy.

You might have seen pictures of early villages with farmers happily going about their business but these don't show how, for the first time in history, people had to live in the middle of all kinds of smelly filth. New bugs came to make their life a misery. Many farmers used irrigation to water crops and this allowed mosquitoes to feast on their lovely juicy bodies. Bed bugs originally lived in caves and drank the blood out of bats. But when humans began building permanent houses the bed bugs thought they were little outdoor caves and moved in to begin feeding on the inhabitants. I don't know if you have ever been bitten by a bed bug but I can tell you from personal experience,

DIRT 25

it is extremely unpleasant and the itchy bites hang around for days. Fleas also saw an opportunity and colonised us after moving off dogs.

Cows, sheep, humans, dogs, chickens, pigs and ducks all make a tremendous amount of excrement. In early settlements there was no way to clear it all up and for the first time humans couldn't move away from it. In fact, they used it to make walls of their houses, fertilise their fields, burn in their fires – it was everywhere. In all animal waste there are eggs from worms and so humans became infested with a whole range of internal parasites, which we will talk about in a later chapter.

Believe it or not, all of this new-fangled farming didn't improve our ancient ancestor's health. People got shorter, developed vitamin deficiency diseases like rickets, wore out limb joints and died about fifteen years younger than their nomadic Ancestors – **RIPPED OFF!**

MEDIEVAL FILTH

There are lots of names for the toilet but one of the most common ones is 'the loo'. It sounds pretty civilised, but this term comes from the French term "guardez le eau" which translates as "watch out below for the water". Obviously these Frenchies were being polite because it wasn't water they were throwing out of their windows. They were getting rid of good old fashioned 'night soil'. 'Night soil' is another polite term for human excrement.

In the Middle Ages the size of human populations grew very quickly. The only other time there had been so many people in Europe was during the Roman Empire. But as you know the Romans were fantastic engineers and built public lavs and sewers and such. The Europeans of the Middle Ages were great at building things like cathedrals that looked after the 'soul' but not so good at building things that looked after 'night soil'.

All they could do was dump it in the street. Some threw it out after yelling 'watch out below' three times, although no doubt many busy housewives didn't have time to and just chucked it out. Medieval men taking their favourite lady out for a hot medieval date were meant to walk on the outside while his lady love walked next to the wall so if there was an unpleasant delivery he'd be most likely to cop it.

And you thought modern first dates were awkward!

Believe it or not some fancy houses had garderobes. Just like in castles, these were structures sticking out from the wall, which even had a toilet seat. This allowed the proud owner to defecate and get rid of the waste into whatever was below. This was fine in castles where the smelly package dropped right into the moat, but imagine walking along a medieval street, being hit in the head by a smelly turd and looking up to see a hairy bum staring down at you.

Not my idea of fun, that's for sure.

Pots full of piss and poo weren't the only things chucked into the street. To fetch and heat water was a time consuming business so, if a family made the momentous decision to have a bath, the oldest would go first followed by the younger members of the family. Eventually the water would become pretty noisesome (smelly) and it too would be heaved out of a window. This gave rise to the term "don't throw the baby out with the bathwater", as of course bubs would the last one in.

DIRT

"Don't throw the baby out with the bathwater."

It wasn't only human waste that gathered, but dead cats, rats and dogs, animal crap, food scraps, old floor straw and thousands of other unmentionables would collect. During the wet seasons this would be okay, as it would wash away, but in a long hot summer it must have been pretty darn horrible. I don't know about you but I certainly would not want to live in London's 'Steaming Lane' or 'Shitburne Street'. In Paris there was a street called 'Rue de Pipi'. Charming.

Fortunately, there was a solution. If you wanted to earn double the regular wage you could become a muckraker, gob farmer or cart man whose job it was to remove the huge amount of filth.

Chucking stuff out of a chamber pot was one thing, but what if you needed to 'attend to business' while you were out and about. There were no public lavs in those days so you had to do it wherever you could. Any convenient alley would do. Women in long skirts would just stop in the middle of the street and let go. One guide to table manners warns that diners sitting down to eat in a public house were advised to check that the previous customer had not 'befouled' the seat and left an unwelcome token of their presence. A German book on good manners wrote that it was rude to relieve themselves 'like rustics' in front of ladies, out of windows or behind doors. A French book explained that it was bad manners to urinate or defecate in 'staircases, corridors or closets'!!! The same book advised that gentlemen should not point out any particularly large poos he might see in the street to his lady. Anybody did it anywhere. King James the First loved hunting so much that he would not dismount from his horse but would urinate while in the saddle.

WASHING CAN KILL

Next time your mom or dad tells you to jump in the bath you can explain that washing is in fact bad for your health. Medieval doctors were convinced that diseases entered through pores in the skin so it was best if they were clogged and filled with blackheads.

The Christian church frowns upon a lot of things even today, but back then you were committing a sin if you got naked to wash. Queen Isabella of Spain was so religious that she only bathed twice in her entire life – when she was born and on the night of her wedding. Queen Elizabeth took a bath once a month whether she 'needed it or not' but didn't brush her teeth as blackened teeth were fashionable. James the First would wash his fingertips with a wet rag but never had a bath because he hated water. French doctors thought that the smell of soap was bad for a patient's health so they recommended dirty bed linen.

Tell you mom this wise old proverb "Wash your hands often, your face seldom and your head never."

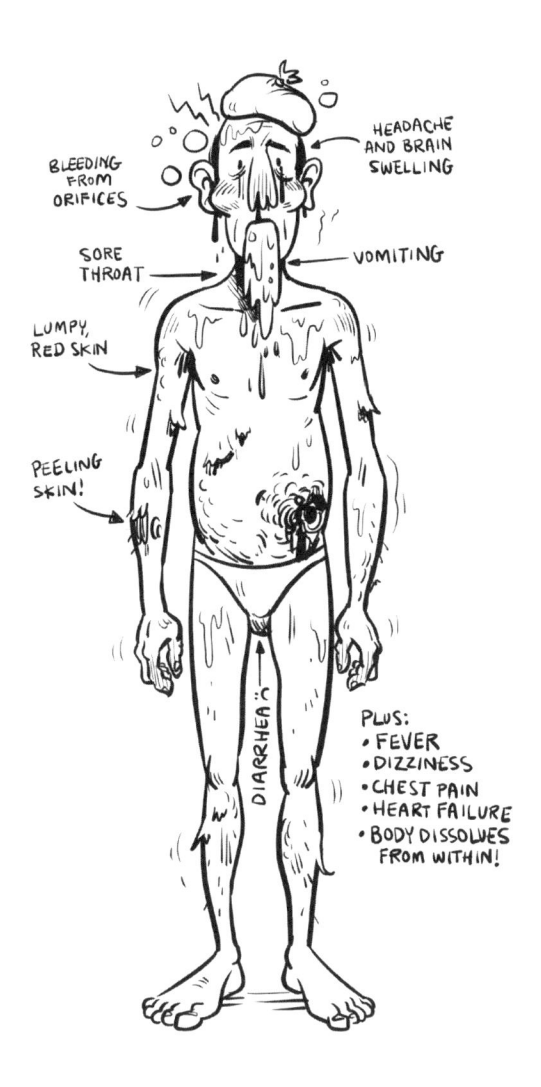

CHAPTER 2

Ebola

The rainforest's revenge

Ebola is a nasty nasty nasty disease. I am sure you people reading this book don't have any enemies; you are no doubt intelligent and very clever. But, even if you did have the worst enemy ever, someone you hated so much that you spent hours at night thinking of all the dreadful things you could do to get even with them, even if you had an enemy like that, you would not want them to get Ebola.

Ebola is a haemorrhagic fever, which means that once you get it you start to leak fluids, such as blood and saliva, out of your body.

The symptoms are pretty horrific so don't read this bit if you have just had a big meal or feel carsick easily.

The Ebola virus is a nasty customer!

EBOLA SYMPTOMS

Once a person or animal is infected it can take up to 24 days for the symptoms to become obvious. This is fortunate because once the disease takes hold the poor patient is going to be on a roller coaster of suffering – but this roller coaster only goes downhill. Usually the disease incubates (builds within the body) for 4 to 10 days. The first symptom is a bit like a cold or flu. A sore throat and headache, which can be joined by a bit of a sniffle, muscle pain and general miserableness. However, at this stage Ebola is setting itself up to create havoc. Not only is every little bit of snot or phlegm contagious to other people but the virus starts to spread into every bit of the host's body.

After five days the flu becomes deadly – the skin is attacked and becomes red and lumpy, sometimes the skin even begins to peel off.

Friends and family usually get a bit scared by this time as the patients' eyes become red and bloodshot and they begin to vomit and have uncontrollable diarrhoea. (I told you it was pretty bad, but it's going to get worse.) Then the poor sufferer gets uncontrollable hiccups along with dizziness, chest pain and shortness of breath.

It is now that the patient enters the most dangerous time – the Ebola virus is so nasty that it begins to liquefy the internal organs and the patient starts to bleed uncontrollably out of their ears, eyes, mouth and other bits that we won't mention.

This leads to blood flow not reaching organs such as the liver, brain and kidneys. The adrenal glands break down and liver and kidney failure follows. The body's connective tissues are also attacked and the body literally dissolves from within. The pancreas is infected and causes severe abdominal pain while the intestines are savaged by the virus. No food or nutrients can be absorbed and massive diarrhoea continues while the patient becomes dehydrated and the brain swells causing splitting headaches.

After 4 to 11 days of suffering, death often occurs as the heart gives way.

That's enough of the symptoms for now, but every bit of fluid, wherever it comes from is a toxic bit of infective material and even the smallest bit can make another person sick.

CATCHING EBOLA

Ebola is so dangerous because everybody tries to look after their sick family and friends. They wash them and try and keep them clean but if a tiny bit of Ebola gets in their mouth or eyes, or even into a little cut they get sick too. Ebola has a high mortality rate of up to 80%. In Africa, Ebola raced through some communities because they used to wash their relatives before burial and then drink the water as a sign of respect.

The virus lives in anything that is wet. Blood, saliva, even ones and twos all carry the deadly cargo of the Ebola virus. Fortunately, it is not yet an airborne virus, but the slightest contact with infected fluids will transmit the disease.

NOT CATCHING EBOLA

Of course doctors and nurses dealing with Ebola patients are well aware that it is very easy to catch. Over a hundred and fifty years a lot of protective gear has been developed to stop infection. You have probably been to a doctors where they put on a rubber glove before examining your sore throat and then throw away the glove – well with Ebola they use **PERSONAL PROTECTIVE OUTFITS** – which are like multiple layer, body sized, rubber gloves!

The first thing that goes on is a surgical cap, which is similar to a balaclava; it covers the whole head except for the eyes. This is one of the most important pieces because we, as humans, touch our faces hundreds of times a day – doctors are trained not to but you never know. This also stops yucky bits lodging in the hair. Next on are the goggles; these are awfully important, just in case the patient sneezes or spurts blood. Then a respirator is put on, which filters the air. Over the top of all of this goes a surgical scrub suit followed by plastic overalls that repel any fluids. Over the feet go rubber boots and two sets of rubber gloves cover the hands and cuff of the overalls. Last on is a waterproof apron.

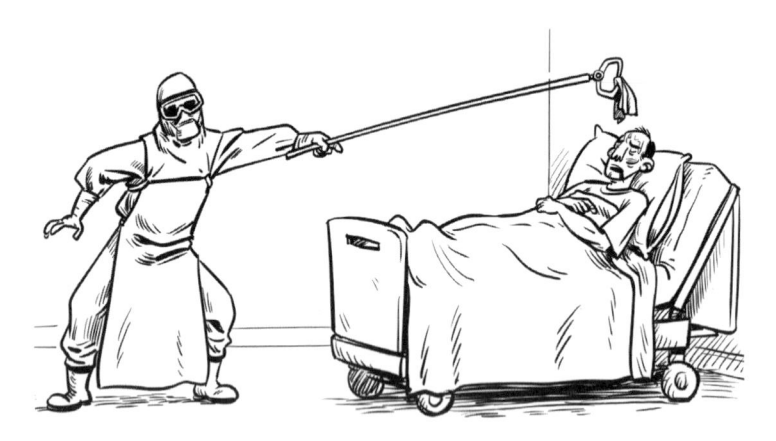

Ebola – handle with care.

As you can imagine, all this takes a heck of a lot of time and once all the gear is on it becomes very hot so most doctors working in Ebola treatment centres can only manage one or two hours before they have to get the kit off. This takes even more time than putting them on. They have to be sprayed with water and chlorine then every piece has to put in a big bucket of disinfectant before it is thrown out. Expensive, time consuming and uncomfortable. But Ebola deserves respect.

WHERE DID EBOLA COME FROM?
THE EBOLA VECTOR

Ebola is the Rainforest's Revenge. For millions and millions of years it has been hiding deep in the jungles of Central Africa. Many different kinds of bats, birds, jungle pigs and rodents have developed a resistance to the virus. Maybe when one of their species was first infected, before our ancestors came down from the trees, they may have died but gradually a resistance was built up. Ebola was just a harmless little bug that may have given these animals a bit of a sniffle but nothing else.

But, last century a new invention changed all that. The invention wasn't particularly fascinating; it wasn't a supersonic train or hadron-collider that could measure the building blocks of the universe. It was much simpler but incredibly destructive – the chainsaw. Maybe thirty years ago the creatures deep in the tropical jungle wouldn't have seen humans, but they would have felt in the air that something had changed. Firstly, they may have heard echoing in the mountains; the rude sound of a chainsaw cutting down mighty forest trees. Then they would have smelt something unusual; the smell of burning wood as vast areas were developed for farmland. Following the chainsaw and the smoke came thousands of people, houses, cars and guns

Then one of these little jungle creatures, a gazelle, was going about its daily business when it heard a loud bang and fell to the ground. A hunter carried his prey to a local village that had just sprung up and sold his 'bush meat' to a school teacher.

This was in August 1976 and the school teacher was Mabalo Lokelat. He lived in a town called Yambuku in the Democratic Republic of the Congo and after eating the meat he began to feel pretty sick. By September 1976 he was dead. But in the underfunded African hospital the needle that doctors used on him was used on other people (the whole hospital only had five needles which they had to re-use!!!). This led to 318 infections and 280 of these poor people died – 90%.

The disease was named after a local river – The Ebola River.

I'm sure you will agree that the Ebola virus is pretty darn nasty. There is good news though – in later outbreaks many countries, including America, Australia and Britain, sent medical help to stop it spreading and knocked it on the head.

But be warned – we have to stop cutting down forests – for thousands of reasons, but also because we never know what is hiding deep in the jungle.

Something's lurking in the forest.

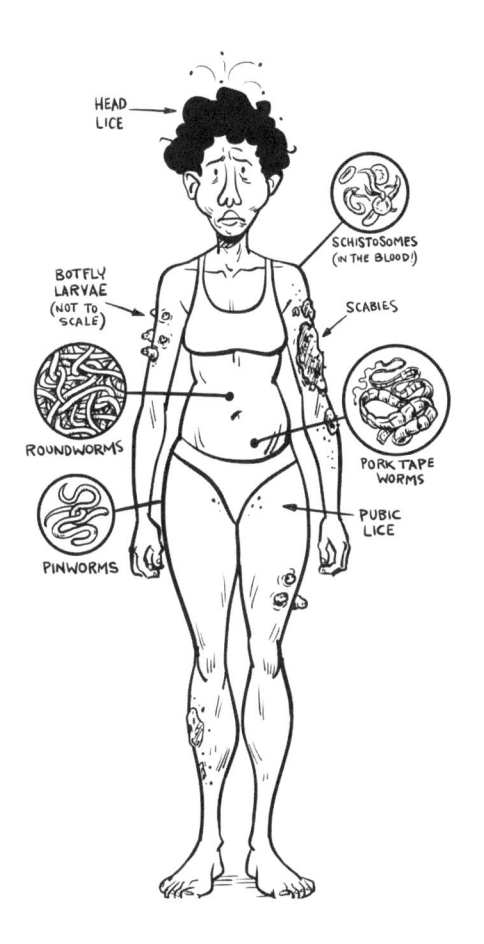

CHAPTER 3

Parasites, Worms & Bugs

Your parents always tell you to wash your hands — here's why!!!

Lindow man was not happy. He was about to be sacrificed and buried in a bog sometime during the 1st Century CE. No doubt Lindow man, let's call him Pete Marsh, knew what was about to happen to him as he'd probably watched a lot of his tribesmen killed in the past. When European men and women were sacrificed to the gods they had to suffer quite a lot. They were strangled, had their throats cut, were beaten about the head and stabbed in the chest. But, if this wasn't bad enough, Pete Marsh had an itchy bum!

Pete Marsh was discovered in Lindow swamp in about 1984. Scientists found that before he was sacrificed he had been to a version of an 'Iron Age Day Spa'. His beard and hair had been neatly trimmed and his fingernails showed signs of a pretty special manicure. After all you can't send a sacrifice to please the Earth Goddess if he's a scruffy bugger. Pete enjoyed a last meal of wheat cake and vegetables as well as some mildly poisonous mistletoe, which might have had the effect of knocking him out a bit.

All of Pete's gut contents were preserved and this included thousands of worms and their eggs. The most common one was the whipworm (Trichuris trichina), which is pretty difficult to get rid of once you have it. These skinny little buggers infest the large bowel (the bit of the digestive tract near your bum) and a female whip worm can live for five years and produce 20,000 eggs a year! These eggs attach themselves to faeces and, if people don't wash their hands after going to the toilet, the worms enter through the mouth and begin to colonise a new host's digestive system. One of the side effects of these nasty little critters is a really itchy bum, especially at night.

But if you think the whipworm was a prodigious breeder it is nothing compared to the other critter that infested our poor victim. The female Round Worm (also known as Maw-worm due to their frightful set of choppers) is much larger than the whipworm and can grow up to 50 cm long with a width of 6 mm. Lindow man was heavily infested and his small bowel (the bit that links the stomach with the large bowel) was packed with male and female maw worms sucking up all of the nutrients before they were absorbed into Pete Marsh's system.

This might have been why Pete was chosen for sacrifice – so many worms make you pale and weak, a perfect subject to dedicate to the gods.

This amazing find proves that various nasty bugs and worms have coexisted with humans for thousands of years. This chapter discusses some of the worst parasitical infections known to man.

OUTSIDE BUGS
PUBIC LICE

We humans are an awful lucky species – we have more kinds of lice than any of our primate cousins! Chimpanzees have head lice and gorillas have pubic lice but lucky old Homo sapiens (you and me) have both kinds. It's best not to think how pubic lice crossed the species divide between humans and gorillas but they are pretty fascinating little critters. Crabs is their other name and it sure is an accurate name.

Nobody wins when they take on this character.

PARASITES, WORMS & BUGS

Unlike other lice or fleas, their legs stick outwards and have hooks at the end so they can swing about in the widely spaced hairs that you probably know as 'pubes'. These nasty beasts don't listen to dieticians who would usually say it is best to have fibre and vegetables in your diet. They only drink blood and feed at the bases of pubic hairs causing an itchy swelling redness. Fortunately, today we can get rid of these bloodsuckers (they can live for days in dirty bed linen) with chemicals. It wasn't that easy in the past when bacon fat mixed with ashes was a suggested cure! What a stink!

BOT FLIES

Don't search 'bot flies' on the internet- it will make you sick, almost as bad as having one yourself. (Don't search 'blackheads' – that's even worse – trust me.)

Many people travel to South America or Africa and pick up a nasty passenger on the way. What started out as an insect bite, a small red lump, gets bigger and bigger and bigger. Then the lump begins to wriggle. It's a bot fly larvae laid just under the skin. These horrible segmented maggots live under the skin with a little hole near their head so that they can breathe. The larvae has a long tail but a body that is barbed like an arrow so that they can't get pulled out of their little hidey-hole.

The only way to get rid of a bot fly is to use a piece of sophisticated medical equipment – sticky tape. At night when an infected host goes to bed they must place the sticky tape over the sore so that their little visitor can't get any air. It takes quite a while for the grub to die and as it slowly asphyxiates is thrashes around making the sore look like a demented psycho-pimple. Finally, after hours of gradually diminishing struggles, the maggot dies and can be pulled out with a pair of tweezers.

Where would be the worst place to have a bot fly grub under your skin do you think? I would hate to have one on the tip of my nose.

Bot flies are 'undeclared luggage'!

SCABIES

Bot flies are bad enough but once they pupate into a fly that is the end of the matter and the poor host# can say goodbye and good riddance. Scabies are an entirely different matter. Once they settle in scabies always cause hours and hours of unbearable itching. The other name for scabies is 'the itch mite'.

'Scabies' probably comes from the word 'scab'. One definition for 'scab' is 'a dry, rough protective crust of congealed blood that forms over a cut or wound during healing'. Scabs can be pretty itchy but scabies are about 200 times itchier because they are made up of millions of tiny mites that burrow into the skin and set up a cosy household. They then begin producing thousands of offspring that eat, live, breed and die until the host's skin becomes a hard crusty surface filled with live and dead mites. As well as dead mites rotting away under the hosts skin they also leave their faeces which is made up of digested human blood. Yowzer!

Mites are probably related to spiders as they have eight legs, but rather than casting webs and sucking the blood out of insects, mites burrow under the skin and suck their host's blood. Scabies burrow into the top level of the skin and lay hundreds of eggs which travel back to the surface of the skin leaving little white trails behind them. They tend to concentrate where the skin is wrinkly; knees, elbows, scrotum and underarms are the favourite hideouts for the nasty little critters.

If that isn't bad enough, full-blown infestations transform into 'the Norwegian Itch'. This is a thick crusty hive of arachnid mites up to half a centimetre thick.

LICE AND NITS

Faster than a speeding snot – it's Super Louse.

'Nits' – this cry is enough to cast terror into the heart of any primary school student. They know that they will not be able to avoid gallons of fouls smelling liquid being scratched through their hair followed by the agonising application of the 'nit comb'.

Nit combs, which have incredibly small gaps between each prong, have been found in ancient graves dating back thousands of years. First Dynasty Egyptians used them regularly as did the Romans. This proves that nits and lice have been around at least as long as the earliest civilisations.

Nits are microscopic eggs that hair-lice lay along the hairs of their hosts. They are usually attached to hairs very close to the scalp. After nine or so days the nit hatches a brand new louse which begins to suck blood and breed. Lice eggs only turn white after they have hatched so the only time they are easy to see is when it's too late. Each female louse lays 5 or 6 eggs a day so it is pretty easy for one little louse to turn into an infestation.

Any mom worth her salt will pour gallons of 'stuff' onto their kid's head to kill the lice infection. 'Off nits', 'Nits off', 'Noffnits' are all likely names for these foul chemical concoctions, but lice have been feeding off human heads for millions of years and they're not likely to give up the gig without a fight.

Nits are becoming resistant to all manner of chemicals so soon a 'SUPER LOUSE' might emerge that will become almost indestructible. The 'SUPER LOUSE' might not be able to stop a speeding bullet but it sure could give you and me an itchy head.

JIGGER FLEA

Jigger fleas are like bot flies, but once they lay their eggs the infection spreads over whole sections of skin. These fleas were originally common in South America, but thanks to the magic of slavery these nasty little sand fleas have colonised most of sub Saharan Africa. A female jigger burrows into the sole of their host's feet and proceeds to lay several eggs. The new jiggers proceed to eat flesh and skin until the whole area becomes a mass of necrotic flesh. The dead flesh, along with its jigger eggs, has to be cut away before gangrene sets in.

INSIDE BUGS
WORMS

Worm eggs usually leave humans and animals when they are pooped out. These eggs often enter humans and animals when they get on food or onto hands and enter through the mouth. They then use all sorts of amazing methods to set up a colony in their new host. While you might reckon it could be pretty horrible to be infested with a whole colony of wriggly nasties, they can in fact have positive side effects. When worms latch onto the inside of you guts some inject a chemical into the host that lowers blood pressure and cholesterol. In some places worms are being given as medicine.

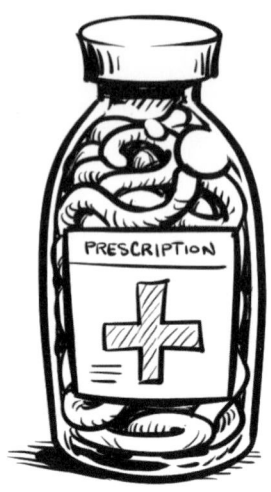

Two spoons a day takes high blood pressure away.

How do they worms evade our immune system? They have evolved with us for millions of years and seem to be able to secrete chemicals which make them invisible to our defenses. Or else our immune system realises that to take on these invaders could cause more harm than good so decides not to pick a fight. Another theory thinks that fighting the worms would lead to a massive inflammatory response that could cause more damage than good.

Have you ever had a big allergic reaction to pollen or cat hair where your nose becomes a river of unstoppable snot – well that might be because of worms – or the lack of worms. Worms have mainly disappeared in modern societies now so our immune systems have nothing to attack. This might have led to modern epidemics of allergies. Crohn's disease, asthma, even diabetes may be the result of lack of worms. These modern diseases are worst where there are no worms.

Crohn's disease seemingly comes out of nowhere and often attacks previously healthy adults. Symptoms are internal bleeding, weight loss, sore throat and cracked lips. The immune system begins to attack the guts. Many patients have been cured of this disease by ingesting worms. These have subdued the immune system, leading to the disease miraculously vanishing. So, as you can see, worms aren't all bad.

This is pretty rare though and most worms are pretty horrible, especially 'tape worms' which are broad and long, just like a bit of tape. It's impossible to talk about all of the worms which infest modern humans but here is a selection of some of the worst. Enjoy!

PORK TAPEWORM

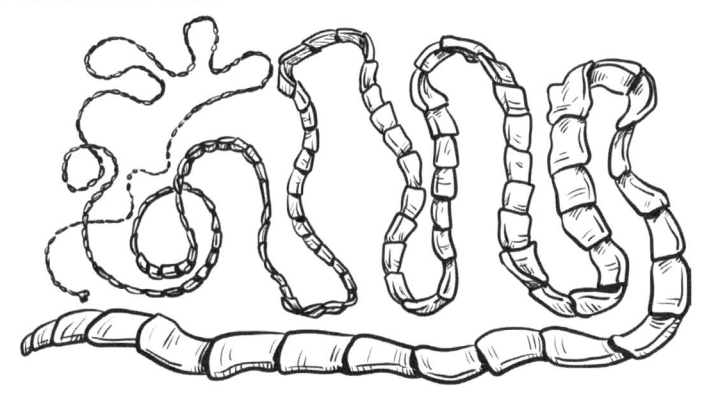

How would you like one of these in your guts?

This is one of the grossest worms ever. Both the Jewish and Arabic religion forbid the eating of pork and this worm might be the reason. It is caught by humans when they eat undercooked pork. The eggs in the undercooked pork meat survive the cooking process and latch onto the human gut where they grow into the monster shown above.

The egg grows into a segmented flatworm that can be up to twenty feet long! As you can see in the picture above, the end of the flatworm is divided into segments. These sections are packed full of new eggs and are actually alive. They can come out of their host when they go to the toilet or else (CODE RED – GROSS OUT ALERT) they can wriggle their way out of your bum while you sleep! If you are awake you'll feel a slight fluttering below your stomach and then a strange feeling as it comes out of your bum and wriggles its way out from between your buttocks before falling down your leg.

If that's not bad enough, if the eggs are ingested on contaminated food they seem to develop a life of their own and penetrate into the blood stream. From here they migrate through the circulatory system into muscles, organs and even the brain. This condition is called cysticercosis. As the eggs set up little cysts and bring on epileptic fits that get worse and worse until the poor old victim keels over and dies. What's worse, they can even play house in your eyeballs!

These worms are pretty common in South America and many American tourists pick them up on their travels. Once lodged in the brain they give similar symptoms to a brain tumour and brain surgeons often find them and use tweezers to extract the unwelcome visitors. More usually though, x-rays show that they are worms and the patient is given drugs that kill the worms, allowing the brain fluids to dissolve the cysts and return to normal.

Each female pork tapeworm can produce up to 50,000 eggs a day and the eggs are pretty tough, they can survive in formaldehyde for up to 2 months.

Fortunately, this tapeworm is not too common anymore and when it is in the gut it can be killed with simple drugs.

TRICHENELLA are another kind of worm that lives in undercooked pork While not as lethal as pork tapeworms, they too have a diabolical trick to get into your guts. When the female lays her eggs they are contained in a tough little sac. This sac is digested in your stomach acids, freeing the worms to get into your intestines. Although they are pretty tiny worms a large infestation can lead to vomiting and stomach cramps.

PARASITES, WORMS & BUGS

PINWORMS

These are the most common kind of worms and they live in the colon and the rectum. Most kids get these worms before they are twelve by ingesting other kids' faecal matter. Whenever you dip your hands into somebodies chip packet or share lollies with your friends, chances are they're popping a bit of poo and some worm eggs into the mix. And this isn't by accident – the pinworms have a cunning plan to spread their eggs.

A bowl of peanuts can be 'DEADLY'.

During the day the pinworms act pretty innocently and feed on bacteria found in your guts. But, once you're asleep, the 13 mm long female pinworms carry out their dastardly plan. They wriggle their way out of your rectum and lay lots of eggs. These eggs irritate the skin making it very itchy so even in your sleep you scratch your bum and get lots of eggs stuck under your fingernails. Even with a decent hand wash some of these eggs stick around, ready to infect the next big bucket of popcorn that your share with your chums. Once the eggs are eaten they head straight to the next person's colon where it all starts over again. I'm sure you'll agree this is a pretty diabolical plan for an animal that doesn't have a brain!

The earliest archaeological record of a pinworm are some eggs found in a coprolite (fossilised faeces) dated to about 8000 BCE in Utah America. Ancient Chinese recommended eating huge amounts of garlic to flush out your system. Hopefully this remedy would work or you'd have really bad breath AND an itchy bum.

SCHISTOSOMES

Worms, grubs and critters that live in your guts are bad enough but these horrific parasites **LIVE IN YOUR BLOODSTREAM**. The schistosomes larvae begin life in water snails before they are released into rivers and ponds. From here they burrow through skin and find their way into your cardiovascular system where they latch on to a vein wall and begin to feed on your blood!

Gut worm vampire.

They can grow up to 15 cm and spend lots of time laying eggs, which are carried into different organs causing all types of trouble. These tricky critters are mainly found in Africa.

ROUNDWORMS

The roundworm is called the roundworm because it is round. This may seem self-evident and a much better name should be 'the nearly indestructible gut sucking killer that currently infests 1 billion people worldwide'. The scientific name is Ascaris lubricoides, although it is also known as the maw worm because of its particularly frightening mouth.

These are particularly nasty worms that can grow to 50 or 60 cm long. They can infest a host's gut in such numbers that they almost clog the entire digestive system and suck up all the nutrients so that their poor victim dies. This is particularly true of children and old people. There's some pretty horrible stuff out there, during the middle ages people reported children's belly's splitting open and hordes of wriggly worms 'spewing forth-with'. Whether this is true or not, roundworms can certainly mess with your insides.

You might have seen an 'Alien' movie where a person has a sucker attached to their face which implants an egg. The egg grows up into an angry little alien that bursts out of the poor person's gut looking like an angry football coach. While it's pretty gruesome this life cycle is simple compared to what a roundworm gets up to.

First a fertilised egg is eaten along with some food. It gets to the stomach where the egg becomes a larval (baby) worm. The larva then penetrates the piece of the intestine just below the stomach (the duodenum) and enters the bloodstream It is then carried around the body visiting the liver and heart before lodging in little air sacs of the lungs called the alveoli. These alveoli are the sensitive bits of the lung which absorb oxygen into the bloodstream and cause you to cough if any smoke or irritant gets in there. The little larva then has a bit of a holiday and grow before they moult and shed dead skin. This irritates the lungs and the host coughs up the little worms into their mouth where they are swallowed and they make their way to the small intestine where they attach themselves to the intestine wall and start feeding, having sex and producing up to 200,000 eggs per day for up to two years!

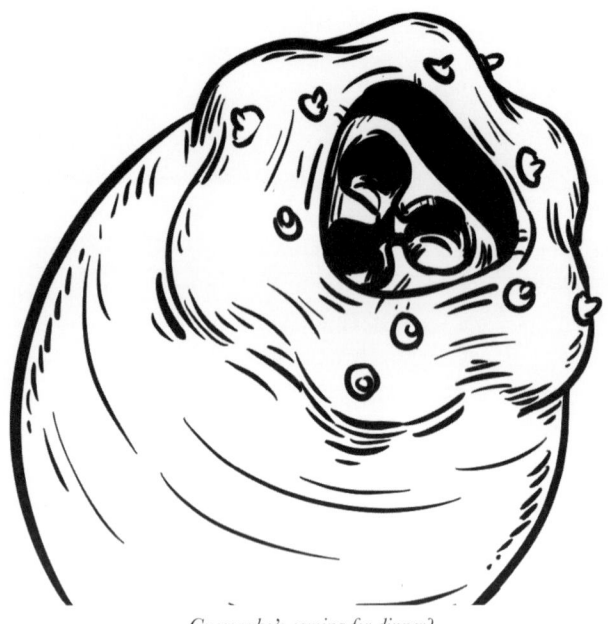

Guess who's coming for dinner?

Why the larva didn't just go straight to the small intestine rather than having a holiday traveling round your bloodstream and airways is a bit of a mystery. Maybe it's just that hanging on to an intestine wall and sucking up vitamins isn't all that fun and the roundworms want to live a little before becoming an adult. A roundworm gap-year perhaps.

Apparently one remedy for round worms is to stop eating. The worms get so hungry that they go looking for food and stick their head out of the host's mouth who can then grab the pesky critter and pull it out. This sounds a bit dodgy to me. It's much easier to go to the local chemist and buy some worming tablets which kill them pretty much straight away. Even better, some of these tablets taste like chocolate.

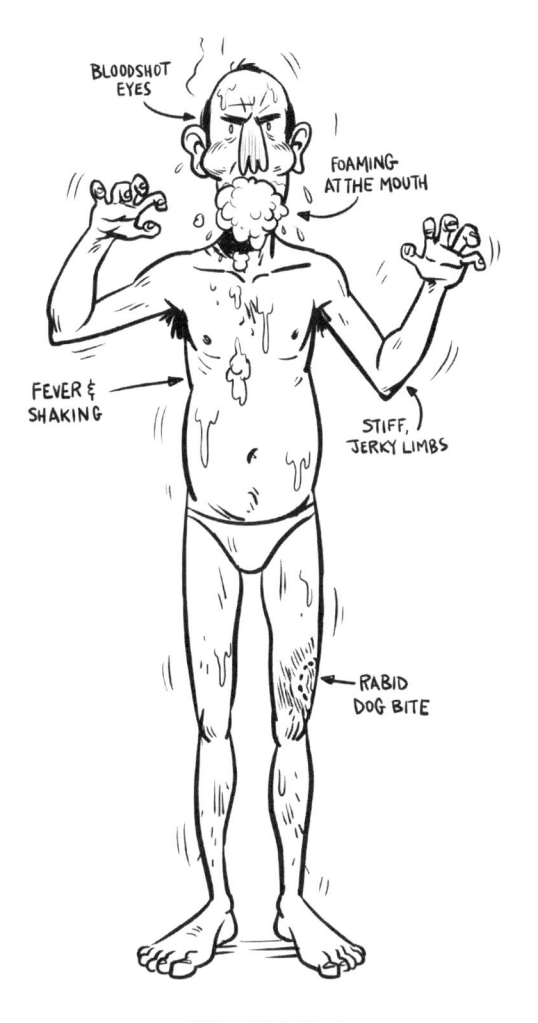

CHAPTER 4

Rabies
Death by dehydration

Imagine a relative you love is bitten by some creature. Let's call your relative 'Aunty Betty'. At first she seems okay but then your beloved aunt's eyes begin to turn red and bloodshot. Betty begins to pant heavily and her skin becomes flushed and spotty. Even worse, she complains of being hot and starts to rip her clothes off, which is pretty darn embarrassing to everybody. Those fingers that used to serve up scones and tea seem to turn into dangerous, and even deadly, talons.

After a short time, Aunty Betty begins to look around crazily and even begins to froth at the mouth with white and blood flecked sputum. Her once loving eyes get a crazed look. In funny jerky motions she staggers towards you. She begins to groan and make funny yelling noises. Her teeth begin to gnash together as if she wants to take a huge chunk out of you.

Your loving auntie Betty has turned from a polite little lady in a frock into a ravening beast!

Has she turned into a zombie?

No. Zombies don't exist.

She has become rabid. Once a person becomes rabid there is no hope – the rabies virus has taken over.

Give Aunty Betty a kiss!

I love dogs and I have two cavoodles. One is called Scruffy and the other is Chester. They are both lovely cute dogs, but if they had rabies I would run a mile. One bite from rabid dog, or even a little nick, can lead to the dreadful, incurable diseases of rabies. Of all rabies infections 99% are caused by 'rabid' dogs.

You can spot a rabid dog a mile away. Huge amounts of phlegm and snot and foamy saliva pour out of their muzzles and nostrils while their eyes are inflamed and red. They are driven absolutely crazy by 'hydrophobia' (a fear of water). They growl and bark and bare their jaws, even if there is nobody or nothing near them (kind of like that crazy person on the train who talks to himself). They pant very loudly, are unsteady on their feet and seem to have a glazed look in their little doggy eyes.

Rabies sufferers are terrified of water.

If you see a rabid dog, you are well advised to steer well clear of it, as it will attack anything close by and give it a very nasty bite.

In this book you have read many diabolical methods that different bacteria, viruses and bugs seek to survive and infect new hosts. But the rabies lyssavirus has a particularly cruel method of tormenting its host. When the poor animal or person has been well and truly infected, the virus starts reproducing in huge amounts within the salivary gland. This is of course the place where saliva is created and soon it is full of the nasty little rabies germs determined to infect a new creature. The saliva begins to foam and pour out like a lemonade slushy. The other symptom is 'hydrophobia' which makes the animal absolutely terrified of even the thought of water and also stops the swallowing reflex. Infected humans who even think of getting a drink experience painful cramps in the throat.

So, as you can see the virus is very cunning. It knows that for a successful infection to take place a large number of the virus must enter the new host's blood stream. It stops the already infected animal from diluting the number of viruses when it prevents it from drinking extra fluid or swallowing.

The rabies virus is very clever.

Rabies has been around for a long time. It seems that humans and dogs first became domesticated maybe hundreds of thousands of years ago, and the disease has probably been in humans since then.

Quite remarkably, a Roman physician who was writing in the first century AD called Aulus Celsus used the word 'virus' to describe the disease. In these books we don't often bang on about special doctors who named things but Celsus made a real contribution. In Latin 'virus' means 'something slimy and poisonous' and ever since then the word has stuck for some of the worst diseases ever. He also realised that the sickness was contained in the dog's saliva and suggested various ways to extract it including 'cupping'.

Celsus was many years ahead of his time; it was not until the 1930s that viruses were seen in electron microscopes.

Other words summed up the disease – 'rabies' is from an Indian word meaning 'to be violent'. The Greeks called it 'lyssa' which means 'frenzy'. The French call it simply 'la rage'.

In the meantime, there were lots of cures to try and help those who were bitten. Some were advised to jump in the sea, others had the wound cauterised, some had electric shocks and others were told to eat the mad dog's liver.

WARNING – WARNING – GROSS OUT ALERT
In Korea they used ground up kittens mixed with alcohol as a cure. Obviously they knew cats and dogs didn't get along very well and it was thought the 'cat medicine' would counteract the 'dog sickness'.

Nowadays there is a cure for the rabies virus if you get bitten. In some Asian and American countries, it is advised to get shots whenever you get a dog bite, whether you think the dog is rabid or not. As long as the antiviral injection is taken within ten days of the bite the infection can be stopped. If not, it is 'all over – red rover'.

Rabies lyssavirus is named after the Greek Goddess 'Lyssa' who is the patron deity for madness, rage and frenzy. Why the Greeks had a goddess for these things is beyond me but it is surely a good name for the symptoms of rabies.

The virus creeps through the victim's nervous system before lodging in the brain. This can take between four days and six years! Once Rabies gets to the brain it begins starting all kinds of mischief. The first symptoms can be a mild fever and generalised aches and pains. This is soon followed by much worse symptoms as rabies causes inflammation of the brain. Blinding headaches, paranoia, panic attacks, paralysis, violent movements, uncontrollable excitement or confusion, hallucinations, screaming, yelling, hydrophobia and an urge to bite everything in range are common occurrences at this stage.

Within 10 days of the first symptoms arising the patient usually falls into a coma before dying.

Rabies was such a horrible disease that in medieval Europe some people would commit suicide or be beaten to death by other villages as soon as the first symptoms arose. In Ancient Mesopotamia you could be executed if your rabid dog infected another free person but you would only be fined if your dog bit a slave.

In medieval times rabid dogs were a threat that had to be eliminated.

Many countries have managed to become rabies free. Foxes in Switzerland used to carry the virus. The clever Swiss didn't want to kill all their foxes so they filled chicken heads with an antiviral medication. The chook heads were scattered around the countryside, the foxes ate the heads, and voila – rabies free foxes.

FACINATING FACT

Rabid patients might have been the inspiration for the modern phenomenon of crazed, mindless zombies who are infected by a single bite. In an amazing twist rabies can also be carried by other animals such as racoons, skunks and bats. These bats include the flying foxes in Australia and the Vampire bats of Central and South America. If rabid they can infect humans and have caused several deaths. Imagine that combination – Vampire Bat Zombies. Or Skunk Zombie stink attack!

Rabies has been removed from many countries and if you take a dog overseas it is likely he will have to spend several weeks in 'quarantine' to ensure it is not carrying the virus.

Skunk zombie

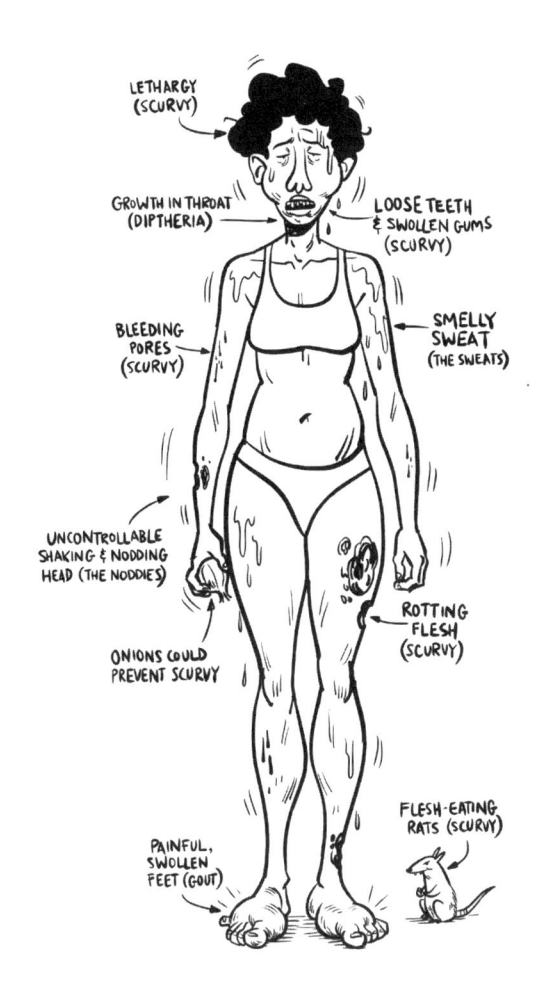

CHAPTER 5

Miscellaneous Maladies
A pocket full of pustules

By now you have probably realised that there are a whole lot of nasties out there, but we have really only touched the tip of the iceberg. Thousands of other diseases exist and lots have been pretty much eliminated. This chapter deals with some of the lesser known or notorious conditions that I hope you never have a personal acquaintance with.

GOUT

Gout is such a painful disease that sufferers would do anything to cure it. One remedy required the patient to cook up a goose stuffed with chopped up kittens, incense, fat, wax and flour. This delightful concoction should then be eaten up all in one sitting. Any fat and dripping was to be rubbed on the affected area. Another well-known cure was to carry a potato in your pocket. I know which cure I would prefer, even though they would be both pretty useless.

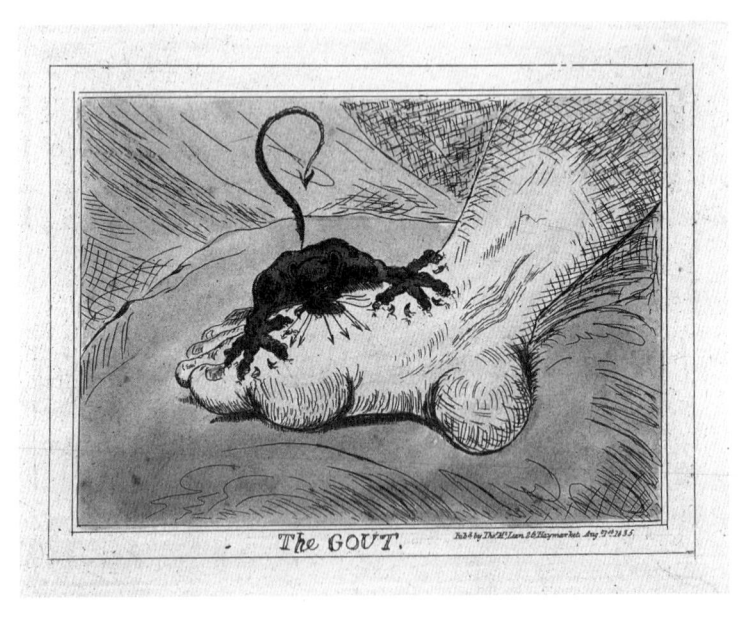

James Gillray painted this picture of the Gout Demon in 1799. He obviously knew how painful it was.

Gout is actually caused by a badly swollen joint, such as a toe bone or wrist bone, which becomes absolutely agonisingly painful. Any attempt to use the offending body part meets with swift retaliation – an agonising stab of pain that seems to travel along the entire nervous system straight into the poor sufferer's brain. Even the tender caress of a sheet placed gently on top of a swollen toe can cause unbelievable suffering. A person who has experienced the agony of gout usually knows the process it takes. A minor stiffness in the joint, another favourite location is the ball of the thumb, slowly gets worse and becomes warm to the touch. The warmth becomes hot and the area becomes red, swollen and extremely painful.

This book is *Disgusting Diseases – A **Young** Person's Guide* so it is likely that you young readers have not suffered gout yet. Count yourself lucky! It mainly affects older people and is caused by a build-up of uric acid which comes from things such as beer, red wine and port. If you have been getting stuck into this kind of thing it might be an idea to stop immediately!

Gout might be the reason that the Romans liked to bash up other peoples. It is guaranteed to turn the kindest person into a raging ogre. Romans used lead pipes. Lead in a human's system means that they are unable to flush uric acid out of the blood. This, combined with their love of red wine, meant that many Romans were effected. Some of the most notorious Roman emperors such as Nero and Caligula suffered from gout.

If it is untreated the uric acid can build up so badly that it causes thick horny growths to build up over the joints and even penetrate the skin. Some Egyptian mummies dated to 4000 BCE show typical signs of the condition. The earliest written reference to gout is found in Homer's Iliad. The Trojan warrior Anchises displeased Zeus who struck his big toe with a thunderbolt. This made the poor bugger unable to walk or fight the Greeks.

If only Anchises had kept off the red wine and eaten less sacrificed bull.

Nowadays, sufferers know to take an anti-inflammatory as soon as that first nasty little twinge raises its ugly head.

Gout has been around for thousands of years – even Mummies had it.

SCURVY

Sometimes you might not feel too important in the grand scheme of things but believe it or not you are composed of 50 to 70 TRILLION cells and every one of those cells reckons you're the bees-knees. Well they have to don't they? Without you they wouldn't exist.

In the time it took you to read that previous paragraph millions of your cells will have died and new cells have been created to replace them. You may have heard the myth that your whole body is replaced every 10 years of so.

Some of this is accurate. Many cells live for only four or five days! They are the cells that have the toughest job to do; your stomach cells are attacked by digestive acids, as are your bowels. Skin cells live for about four months, as do blood cells which have a big job picking up oxygen and emptying it out thousands of times a day. Lung cells live for about two to three weeks. Bone cells can live for seven to ten years. However, the longest living cells are your brain cells – they live for your whole life. As you get older they die off and that's when you lose your marbles. The heart cells replace themselves every twenty years or so.

As you can see your body is an amazing cell producing machine. But it needs one absolutely vital ingredient if it is to create new cells – this ingredient is ascorbic acid, which you know as vitamin C.

Without your daily dose of oranges or vegetable your body can't make new cells and the symptoms of scurvy appear.

MISCELLANEOUS MALADIES

The first sign of scurvy might be when an old wound or cut that you had many years ago mysteriously opens up and begins to bleed. Or else it might be when a pesky pimple that you thought was well and truly gone turns red and fills up with pus-again! This is because where there are old wounds the skin is a little bit thinner and once your cells start to die off these wounds reopen first. These sores start to stink and bits of skin can even start rotting away. As can be guessed, another symptom of scurvy is a foul noxious odour bad enough to make even your mom go "Phew – you stink!".

Another sure sign you haven't been eating your vegies is when gums begin to swell and teeth become loose, blood comes out of pores or hair follicles and you start feeling incredibly tired and lackadaisical. There are many stories from the Age Of Exploration (1500–1800AD) of sailors who are so affected by scurvy that they couldn't be bothered fending off hungry ship's rats that came up to eat their rotten flesh.

The sailors of this time had little understanding of what caused scurvy and hundreds of thousands died from this disease – especially if their sailing ships were becalmed in the middle of the ocean with no access to fresh food. Ferdinand Magellan's expedition around the globe in 1519 started off with 250 men but only 18 survived – most had died of scurvy.

Luckily for sailors everywhere James Lind (1716–1794) worked out that fresh fruit could cure sailors. The death rate was cut incredibly quickly. The first Fleet to Australia in 1778 saw everybody being issued with as many raw onions as they could eat. None got scurvy. Their breath must have been pretty bad though. Maybe it should be called 'The Halitosis Fleet'.

The Halitosis Fleet – 'Stay on board sailor!'

MISCELLANEOUS MALADIES

DID YOU KNOW
THE SWEATS

One of the most mysterious diseases ever was 'The Sweats'. It was an absolutely dreadful disease that came out of nowhere and could strike the strongest person down in less than 24 hours. Most who became sick died. Unlike many infectious diseases it wouldn't wipe out whole families but would strike like lightning and only strike one unfortunate individual.

It's lucky for you and me that 'The Sweats' is no longer around and seems to have disappeared for ever.

It was also known as the 'English Sweate' and first hit England in 1485. An attack began with a feeling of slight anxiety. Well-deserved with what was to come. It was followed by cold shivers, a headache, giddiness and very sore shoulders, limbs and neck.

This lasted for two hours and then the whole body went into meltdown. The patient's body turned into a furnace and poured out a noxious smelling sweat that made all around want to gag. The heart rate soared so that the chest beat like a drum. They sweated so much that all the poor person could think of was drinking water.

Then came the most serious stage of all. The poor person suddenly became incredibly sleepy and just wanted to drift off. Their family knew though that if they let their loved one fall asleep – they would never wake up. Whole families would carry the patient around, hit pots, sing songs and even burn them to try and keep them awake. This did not always work and many thousands of Englishmen died. At one stage it leapt the channel and infected thousands of Europeans even reaching as far as Switzerland.

The last reported death from 'The Sweats' was in 1551. Then it disappeared into the history books.

The Sweats strike – in 20 hours you're gone.

MAD COW DISEASE

Can you think of one thing on earth that doesn't share our DNA? DNA is the building block for every single thing that lives on earth. (Some theories say that we are just vehicles for DNA without free will or independent thought – spooky.) Anyway, every plant, animal, bacteria and virus has some form of link to DNA except for two things – yeast and prions. Yeast is really good as we use it to make bread. It's the agent that makes the bread rise and be all fluffy. It is also used to make beer although I'm sure none of you are interested in that kind of thing.

Prions are an entirely different matter. They are nasty and you don't want them anywhere near you – especially not in your spinal column! Once they lodge in there they migrate to your brain where they start 'bending the proteins' in your brain cells turning it into a spongy mass of dead tissue.

It sounds pretty bad but you don't have to worry too much about getting this condition. Not unless you live deep in the heart of the Papua New Guinean rainforest and eat your dead relatives rather than burying them!

'Noddy' can refer to two things. One is an imaginary character who drives around with Big Ears in a little red car. The other is 'the noddies' – a disease that used to occur to remote tribesmen in remote Papua New Guinean jungles.

When young tribespeople were first struck by the disease they didn't seem sick at all. They would smile and laugh and begin nodding their head. This nodding soon became uncontrollable which led to the name of the illness 'The Noddies'. It usually affected young children or people in their twenties. Eventually the symptoms got a lot worse and the poor people began shaking uncontrollably. The natives' other name for the disease was 'kuru' which means 'the shakes'. At the same time the person became disorientated, had bad mood swings and lost the ability to swallow. Soon the poor person became unable to look after themselves or communicate and would eventually die.

European researchers conducted tests on the victims and found that they were suffering from a prion based infection. It had entered the people's systems and eaten away at the part of the brains that controlled movement. This led to the shaking and the other pretty horrible set of symptoms.

But where did the disease come from? Some tribes would lose hundreds of their young people while a tribe right next to it didn't get any infections at all. They shared the same water sources and even the same animals.

The researchers were determined to find out the cause, but for several years had no luck. But then there was a breakthrough. One person from the infected tribe shared a sacred bit of secret knowledge. When a tribe member died they paid their respects by eating part of the dead body. The tribes thought that if you ate part of the body their relative's spirit would live on. The brain was especially important and it was often fed to the young children so the spirit could live even longer!

Gramps comes to tea.

I'm not sure if the spirits lived on but this practice certainly gave the prions a new lease of life.

In the west this has other names – Creutzfeldt-Jakob disease for humans. Mad Cow disease for, you guessed it, cows. And Scrapie for sheep. When sheep got it one symptom was they would 'scrape' their bums against the ground until their skin and wool were scraped off.

DID YOU KNOW
THE CHOKING DISEASE – DIPTHERIA

In probably the most ironic event in history, Spain experienced an epidemic of diphtheria in 1613. The year was known as El Año de los Garrotillos (The Year of Strangulations) in the history of Spain. It's ironic because The Spanish used to use the 'garrote' to execute their criminals. This particularly nasty device consists of a wooden chair with a neck brace and a large screw. When the screw is turned it would close the prisoner's throat stopping them from breathing.

The garrotte – guaranteed to give you a sore throat.

This is almost exactly how diphtheria works. The bacteria is swallowed or breathed in by the new patient and after about seven days they begin to develop a sore throat, a cough and difficulty swallowing. If the disease progresses then the toxins released by the bacteria lead to a thick brown membrane growing at the back of the throat. The word for diphtheria comes from the Greek word for leather. The growth at the back of the throat is like having a big bit of leather stopping the patient from breathing. In 20% of cases children under 5 years old die from this symptom combined with swelling in the neck.

Fortunately, you don't have to worry about this disease because in most countries it is compulsory to get an inoculation. The first successful inoculation was carried out using a guinea pig in 1890 and the first inoculation of a person took place in Berlin in 1891. Doctor Von Behring won a Nobel prize in 1901 for his work developing a vaccine.

DID YOU KNOW
THE TOOTH WORM

Archaeologists are always amazed at how healthy the teeth of early hunter gatherers are. Rarely do our ancestors display tooth decay. This is no doubt due to the healthy diet of fruits, nuts, vegetables and meats that they gathered during the day. However, once people settled in farming communities they began eating a lot more carbohydrates from grains, which led to many more cavities.

The Sumerians who set up the first known civilisations in the middle east were obviously struck by this disease. They thought it was the work of a 'tooth worm' which penetrated the tooth and set up shop there causing much pain and agony.

Belief in the tooth worm persisted right down to modern times. Sufferers tried to kill the tooth worms by smoking them out or suffocating them by stuffing the cavity with bees wax, partridge brain or crow dung!

The Chinese were the first to invent a useful filling and invented silver amalgam fillings thirteen hundred years ago.

Europeans had another way of curing tooth ache – you had to touch the tooth with a piece of a hangman's noose!

The Australian aborigines had a very practical way of curing a sore tooth. They heated a bit of barbed wire over a fire and jam the red-hot end into the cavity. This kills the nerve and stops any pain.

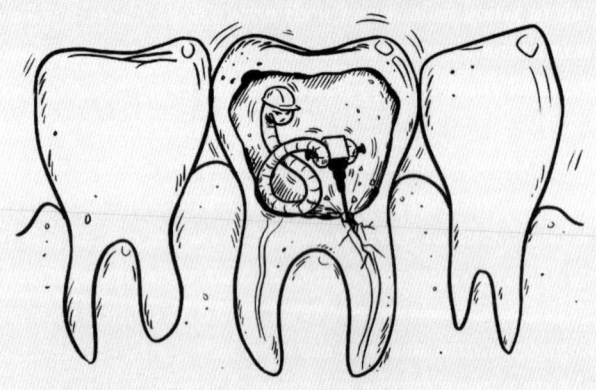

Tooth worms love sugar.

MISCELLANEOUS MALADIES

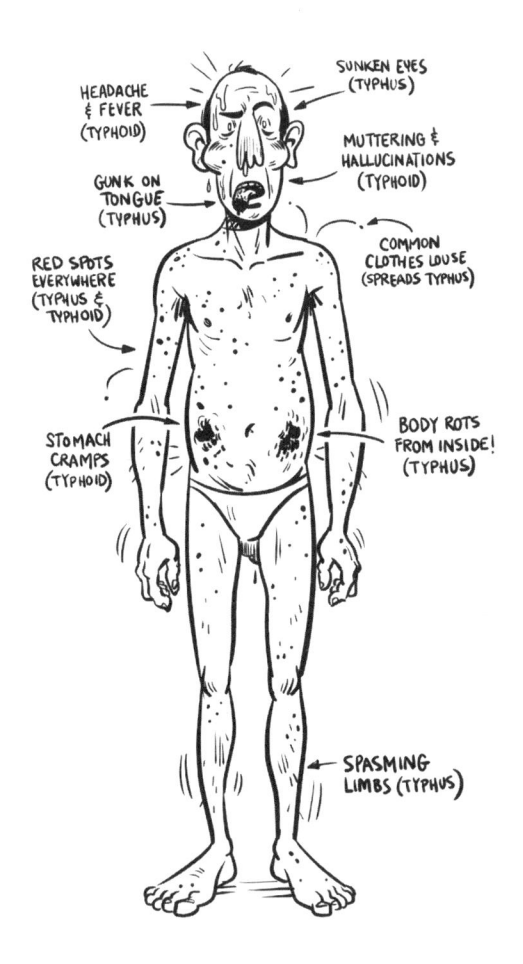

CHAPTER 6

Typhoid And Typhus
The terrible twins

As soon as you saw this chapter heading you no doubt wondered why these diseases were lumped into the same chapter when they are crazily different diseases!

Well, I've written several books on diseases, torture and a whole lot of nasty things, but I always get these two diseases mixed up. If I wack the two in the same chapter maybe, I'll finally manage to stop being confused and maybe you can too.

TYPHOID FEVER

The best way to get into this rather nasty disease is to look at Typhoid Mary. Mary was a great cook, and a very attractive young lady to boot. Mary had great references and never had any trouble getting a job as a cook in posh households of New York.

Her favourite recipe was Peach-cobbler which involved Mary slicing up lovely bits of juicy peach, placing them in a bowl and slathering them with ice-cream and nuts and lots of other lovely ingredients. There was one small problem.

Typhoid Mary was lovely but didn't believe in soap.

Mary didn't like washing her hands. She was also a 'carrier' of typhoid. When After doing a number-two Mary would wipe her bottom, but she would not wash her hands. As she was mixing up the lovely peach cobbler ingredients she was also mixing up tiny bits of faeces along with a fair sample of the bacteria Salmonella typhi. Her poor customers wolfed down the delicious dessert without knowing that it included Mary's 'secret ingredient'.

Not all of the people who Mary cooked for got ill, but quite a few did, and some even died. The first signs that not all was well started a few days after eating the dessert. They would start with cramps in the belly which got steadily worse and worse. Things got even tougher when the poor person developed a splitting headache and a temperature that lasted for up to two weeks. This high temperature would be interspersed with cold chills. Typhoid's aim was obviously to confuse the poor patient. Sometimes they would have 'pea soup' diarrhoea (I'm not going to describe this in greater detail) and at other times they would be constipated. The sufferer then became a bit delirious. They'd mutter, see strange things that nobody else could and pick at their bedclothes as if there were a whole lot of bugs there. This strange behaviour led to the other name for the condition – 'nervous fever'. In the old days 'nervous' was a polite way of saying 'bonkers', 'crackerjack', or 'mad as a march hare'.

If Mary's poor customers went into the third week without getting better, things would get 'pretty serious'. The first sign things were getting dangerous were red spots appearing all over the body followed by dehydration, bronchitis and internal bleeding.

Things were 'really serious' when the patient slipped into a coma and died.

Mary moved from job to job. Quite often she left a trail of death and illness behind her. No doubt when somebody got crook she thought 'oh oh Skeddadle-eeo' and took herself off to another job somewhere else.

Mary didn't have to worry about getting sick, as she was what is known as a 'carrier'. Rather than making Mary sick the Salmonella typhi set up shop in her pancreas and had a bit of a holiday, not affecting Mary at all! Occasionally the bacteria would get sick of hanging about doing nothing and would start breeding furiously. They moved into her digestive system, into her poo, under her fingernails and finally end up in the delicious dinners that she loved cooking up for her admiring customers.

Guess who's coming to dinner! Germs like to hide under our fingernails!

FASCINATING FACT
TYPHOID THE KING KILLER

Archaeologists have found the skeleton of Phillip II of Macedon. They have found out that he looked exactly as described by ancient writers. He had a gammy leg caused by a spear thrust to his knee, and a sword slash over his face that took out his eye. Phillip was the father of Alexander the Great – the greatest warrior in history. We don't have Alexander's body to do an autopsy, but the symptoms that were recorded at his deathbed are similar to Typhoid. The 32-year-old King suffered from chills, exhaustion, sweats, high fever and severe abdominal pain. He died in Babylon where sewerage was mixed in with the main source of drinking water – the Euphrates River.

For some reason ancient people preferred wine to water.

Prince Albert, who was Queen Victoria's husband, died from Typhoid although it was called 'bowel fever'. Even though she was the most powerful woman in the world, when her husband got sick in 1861 she couldn't save him. He died after severe vomiting and diarrhoea on 14th December 1861.

TYPHOID AND TYPHUS

TYPHOID MARY GETS A LIFE SENTENCE

Mary's comeuppance came when she caused an outbreak in the household of a rich banker, Charles Henry Warren, in 1906. The family was living in a huge expensive house in Oyster Bay, New York that they had rented from Mr George Thompson. The family moved in in 1906 and almost immediately six members of the household were struck down with typhoid. The Warrens were not very happy. They thought the water system had caused the outbreak and asked for their money back. Mr Thompson, the landlord, knew he couldn't rent the house again until he found the real cause so he hired the crack private investigator and engineer George Soper to find the real cause.

Soper quickly honed in on the cook as the likely cause and investigated Mary Mallon's past jobs. He found that all of her customers since 1897 had been visited by typhoid fever. Many had eaten her best dish – freshly sliced peaches on top of ice-cream. In fact, after she left the Warren household it is likely that she caused the death of her new employer's daughter.

Soper realised things were pretty serious. By this time the New York authorities knew all about typhoid carriers and Soper wanted to test Mallon to see if she was a typhoid carrier. But first he had to get a sample of her poo, wee and blood.

Easier said than done.

He knocked on Mary Mallon's front door and, in a very polite manner, asked to accompany her to the toilet so that he could obtain the samples. He explained that she could be a carrier of a lethal disease and she may have infected dozens of people with the dangerous typhoid fever.

Now, you can trust me when I say I've never had some random Joe-Blow knocking on my door asking to go to the toilet with me so that he could obtain samples of my ones and twos before he stuck a needle in me to draw blood samples. That would be bad enough, but if I were then told I had infected hundreds of people, I'd expect to be pretty upset.

Mary Mallon was more than upset. Although she was a pretty

woman with big, brown eyes and lovely auburn hair, she seemed to transmogrify into a hideous rage filled harridan. She seized a sharp carving fork and a heavy-duty frypan and raced at Soper, screaming with anger.

Mary was determined not to wash her hands.

The civil engineer and private detective bolted down the corridor and out of the front gate. He probably considered himself lucky to have escaped with his life. Mary then stuck her head out of the window and abused Soper while hurling potato peelings and carrot heads in his general direction.

Soper was not to be put off. He sent a party of five policemen and an ambulance to seize the poor woman. She was ready and waiting and after attacking the posse with her carving fork, bolted into a hidey hole. The constables turned the house upside-down. After searching for an hour or so the police found her huddled in the back of a cupboard. Mary came out fighting like a tiger and the police had to sit on her as she was taken to the hospital for tests.

Her number twos were tested 163 times and most revealed huge amounts of the typhoid bacilli. She was told that she was a 'carrier' and ordered not to work as a cook.

Up until now Mary was a pretty innocent person. Not a lot of people knew about the cause of typhoid fever and no doubt Mary was disappointed to hear of her diagnosis. She was locked up by the New York Health Department until she agreed not to work in a kitchen. She agreed and got a job working in a laundry.

Soon after, there was a massive typhoid outbreak at a hospital in Manhattan. Twenty-four people got seriously ill and two died. The cook, who had renamed herself Mrs Brown, turned out to be Mary Mallon. That is when she earned the name 'Typhoid Mary'. She was hauled off to a secure medical facility where she couldn't do any more damage and she died there in 1938.

If only Mary had learned to wash her hands.

Typhoid fever is still pretty common in countries that don't have good clean water supplies. It's not that dangerous if detected and treated quickly.

TYPHUS

Typhus has many names. Jail fever, ship fever, camp fever and hospital fever. What do all of these places have in common? In the past it was where people were crammed together in insanitary conditions.

When you go to hospital the place is pretty much guaranteed to make you healthy. Even as recently as 150 years ago being sent to hospital could be a DEATH SENTENCE. Mainly in part thanks to the typhus bacteria – Rickettsia typhus and its special friend Pediculus humanus corpori. – the common clothes louse.

Humans are darn lucky – we have three kinds of lice. This is all thanks to evolution. We used to have only one kind of body louse that was pretty much everywhere, but as we became hairless, lice had to decide where to live – in our head hair, in our pubic hair or in our clothes. Of course the Pediculus humanus corporis chose to live in our clothes. Originally furs and then fabrics. These are nasty little critters.

During the day, the clothes louse hides in the seams of our clothes, then at night while we're sleeping it comes out and starts to suck blood. (These lice are confined to humans and if they try to suck some other animal's blood they will die.) They then lay hundreds of thousands of nits on the clothing fibres which hatch into other nasty little lice. If they are not controlled your clothes can almost seem to pulsate with lice.

Thousands of years ago the typhus bacteria hitched a lift into the lice and used them to spread into humans. Their survival strategy is diabolically clever. They live in the lice's guts and when the lice do a poo the faeces are filled with bacteria. The poor old suffering human is so itchy that they scratch their skin so badly that they become covered in scratches and sores. The lice faeces get into these cuts and the bacteria gets into the human's blood stream.

The typhus bacteria hitch a ride on lice to reach our blood stream!

That's not all; one of the first symptoms of typhus is when the infected person gets a temperature. Lice die if they get even slightly warmer than usual so they start leaving the original person's clothes and migrate en-masse onto the next person where the whole process starts again.

I reckon that is a pretty clever survival strategy. It explains while sailors crammed in ships, prisoners locked together in jails, soldiers fighting in trenches, and the sick lying together in hospitals can be decimated and die in their thousands.

There are other survival strategies employed by these brilliant bacteria. The lice put out almost their body weight in faeces every week or so. If it is allowed to dry it becomes a fine powder which can be breathed in and infect the lungs. The bacteria can live for up to two years in discarded clothes, so if somebody puts on the clothing of dead people they can get infected as well.

Some people say that Napoleon would have stayed as emperor if his soldiers hadn't got typhus in 1812.

SYMPTOMS

The word 'typhus' comes from the Greek word 'typhos', which means hazy or confused. This is the first sign that the bacteria had got into somebody's bloodstream. They had cold like symptoms and a bit of confusion for a day or so before they felt better.

But deep inside the body things weren't getting better, they were getting a whole lot worse!

The bacteria entered millions of cells and within each cell they replicated before bursting out and continuing their deadly work. Typhus targeted the cells in the veins effectively killing off huge parts of the circulatory system. This meant that large bits of flesh and skin were not getting oxygen and began to die off.

The poor victim basically rots from the inside.

The first signs that 'things are crook in Tootgarook' were red dots breaking out all over the skin. This gave the disease its other common name – spotted fever. They were followed by a terrible headache, joint pain, sore muscles, confusion and intense fevers. Many patients would strip off their clothes and wander about, babbling mindlessly or acting as if they were at home with mom of dad. Any bright light caused dagger like shooting pains in the eyes. As blood vessels closed down gangrene would set in on the exposed bits like the nose, fingers and toes.

The poor patient became a noxious, smelly, raving, rotting madman! Not nice.

Their tongues became covered with a thick, smelly gunk and their eyes seemed to shrink back into their faces like a cadaver.

They began to pant like mad things or cough uncontrollably as the lungs desperately tried to get extra oxygen into the ravaged veins. Others had spasms when their legs and arms jolted and kicked violently.

By this stage the lice had already jumped off and attacked new people.

Soon after, the patient seemed to get better. Their bodies cooled and they lay still and calm. Experienced doctors knew this was a final calm before their patient died.

I'm sure you'll agree; we are darn lucky that we have antibiotics that can keep us safe from typhus.

HIGH VOICE

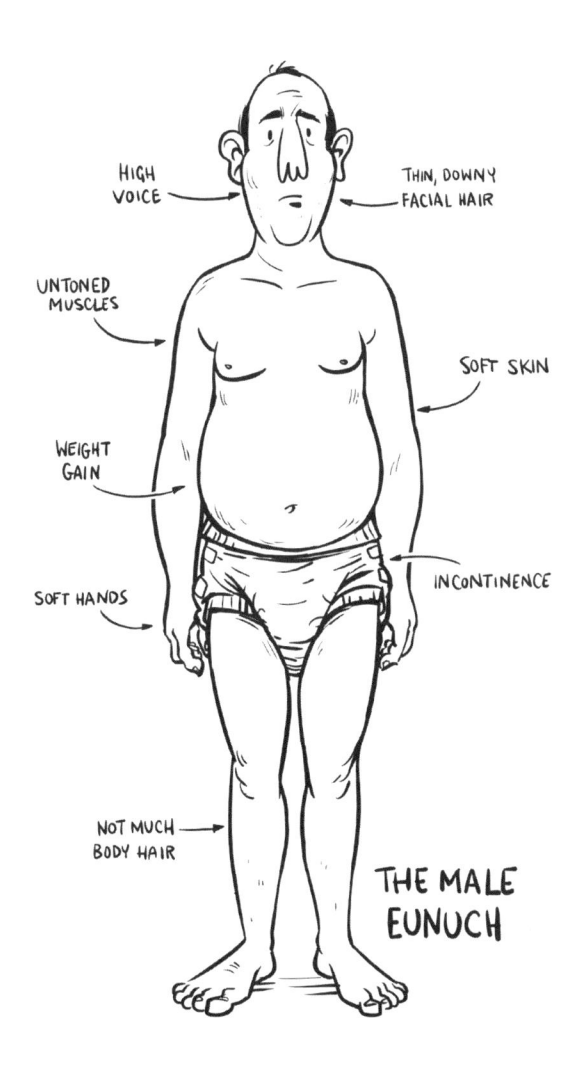

THIN, DOWNY FACIAL HAIR

UNTONED MUSCLES

SOFT SKIN

WEIGHT GAIN

INCONTINENCE

SOFT HANDS

NOT MUCH BODY HAIR

THE MALE EUNUCH

CHAPTER 7

Crazy Cures
Guaranteed to knock you out — forever

What you are about to read is pretty amazing stuff but I can assure you it is all true. At first even I didn't believe in some of these things. There are a whole lot of books out there that say things like 'Hitler is alive and living on the dark side of the moon' or else 'he has been cloned to make a new race of super Hitlers that will come out of Argentina and conquer us all!'.

Straight away you can tell, that kind of stuff is not likely to be too accurate.

A lot of things you'll read in this chapter are pretty farfetched but I read it in quite a few books so you can take it as a cast-iron-guarantee that all of these cures used to be pretty popular.

A good example of this is a cure for sore eyes. Nowadays if you had runny red eyes you'll get some eye drops from the local pharmacy. If you were living in the middle ages, you'd be just as likely to go to the local apothecary who'd sell you some specially prepared dried baby poo and they'd even blow it into your eyes! Difficult to believe? Read on.

An appointment with an 'Apoothocery'.

FACINATING FACT
THE FIRST ANTISEPTIC – URINE

For thousands of years doctors have banged on about how fresh steaming urine is perfect for cleaning wounds. Even though they didn't know about germs, experience showed that washing a new wound in urine, or getting somebody to wee on the wound, stops infection getting hold. Urine is salty and warm and sterile, so when it covers a new wound it washes away impurities and kills a whole range of bacteria that might otherwise cause lots of problems later on. On European battlefields in the later Middle Ages and into the Renaissance, it was common for soldiers who had flesh wounds, particularly on the legs and arms, to ask their comrades to urinate on them.

Pliny the Elder was a natural philosopher in ancient Rome who was so fascinated with the eruption at Pompeii that he sailed close to the eruption so that he could observe it. (Before this eruption in 79 CE Romans had no words for volcano.) Sadly, he collapsed from a heart attack on a beach as the hot gasses surrounded him, but before that he wrote many books on things like natural history and medicine. Pliny, like a lot of Romans, thought urine was a must have in the medicine cupboard.

One recipe was to store urine until it became particularly smelly and then mix it with burnt oyster shells. This paste could cure a whole range of ills. According to Pliny it could cure running sores, itchy bums, skin rashes, cracked skin and scorpion bites.

Pliny went on to write how soda mixed with urine could cure sores around the genitalia, head wounds and dandruff. Personally I'd prefer to walk around with a bit of dandruff rather than walk around with old caked-on wee on my head. What about you?

Urine could cure your dandruff but it would kill your love life.

PHRENOLOGY

Pseudo-Science means a something which sounds like science, looks like science, feels like science, but isn't science. It isn't SCIENCE because it is based on an idea, which is stupid and ridiculous.

A Pseudo-Scientist (P-S) will take this idea and dress it up to look like it's real. He will write learned papers about the subject, draw pretty convincing diagrams explaining it and basically bang on about it so much that it makes mugs like you and me a bit embarrassed to say it's all a load of codswallop.

One of the best known of these P-Ss was the practice of Phrenology. Practitioners thought they could determine a person's personality by feeling around a person's head and mapping all of the bumps, crannies and nooks that were there. Pretty 'harmless' you might think but this 'harmless' craze led to graves being dug up and corpses of famous writers and artists being decapitated so that fanatical Phrenologists could examine their bumps!

Phrenology was invented by a German called Franz Joseph Gall who wrote his landmark book in 1809. The book was titled The Anatomy and Physiology of the Nervous System in General, and of the Brain in Particular, with Observations upon the possibility of ascertaining the several Intellectual and Moral Dispositions of Man and Animal, by the configuration of their Heads. You can tell this is a Pseudo-scientific tract because by the time you've finished reading the end of the title you've forgotten what the start was talking about. It's all very confusing so it must be pretty scientific and accurate.

In this book Gall wrote from his many years of observations how certain parts of the human brain determined certain activities. If you had a big bump over the area that made a person loving, the big bump meant you were very affectionate and kind. However, if you had a big bump over the part of the head that led to violence – people had better watch out or they might get a belting.

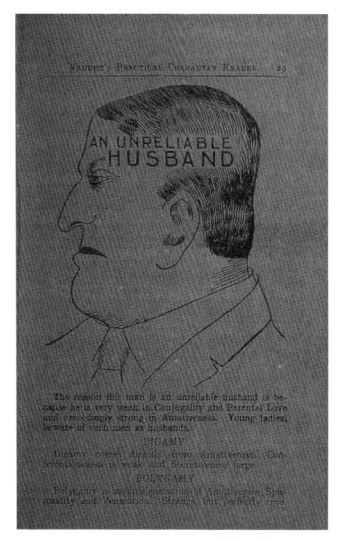

That bloke on the left looks pretty dodgy.

While Gall treated the matter 'scientifically' it soon became a craze and swept through Europe and England, and even into America. Millions of pamphlets were printed, hundreds of thousands of books dealing with the practice were sold, wall posters went into countless homes along with little model busts showing the main regions of the brain. Queen Victoria and Prince Albert arranged to have their children's heads read but it is not known if the famous British Phrenologist, Andrew Combe, managed to get his hands on the royal scalp. The Phrenological society of Edinburgh was founded and soon these learned societies sprang up all over the Western world.

Thousands of Phrenologists set up shop and soon people were booking to have the inner workings of their mind examined. Once in the chair the Phrenologist would run their bare finger tips over the patient's head feeling for bumps or indentations. In some cases, they could whip out some scary looking calipers or make precise measurements with a tape measure. In the 1820s and 1840s some employers demanded a reference from a trained 'head reader'.

It all seems pretty harmless, but Phrenologists set off a crime wave of head hunting – corpses would be dug up, their heads were removed, the flesh was boiled off and a practitioner would have another skull to add to his collection.

This was the fate of Joseph Haydn, the famous Austrian composer. When Haydn died in Vienna in 1809 his good friend Joseph Carl Rosenbaum, who was a music lover and Phrenologist, wanted the composer's head. Rosenbaum bribed the grave digger in the local cemetery to dig up the composer and obtain the head. Rosenbaum was a clever customer. He had already done a practice run by obtaining an actress's head from the grave. He bribed the same grave digger to do this a year or so earlier when Haydn fell ill.

Haydn's skull, the site of so much musical creativity, was mounted on a beautiful black case and topped with a golden lyre. Only in 1954 were Haydn and his head reunited.

Haydn's head – where are the snowflakes?

One other famous soul who had his head stolen was the sadistic sex maniac 'The Notorious Marquis de Sade'. The less you know about this nasty piece of work the better. When his skull was cleaned of its skin, hair, flesh and assorted gooey bits, a phrenologist gave it a reading and determined that it belonged to an exceptionally nice man who would find happiness working in the church and spending his time doing good deeds that didn't involve any sexy things at all!!! This was quite the opposite; de Sade's name is actually the root word for the term 'sadist', which means someone who loves inflicting pain (like your maths teacher).

Fritz Joseph Gall was, even though a bit mad, basically harmless. Even if a Phrenologist didn't really tell you much at least you got a head massage.

TESTICLE GRAFTS

Another pseudo scientist was an entirely different kettle of fish. Dr. Serge Voronoff TRANSPLANTED MONKEY TESTICLES INTO MEN. Voronoff was an ambitious surgeon who wanted to make a name for himself in his adopted country, France. As you may know (or if you didn't you do now) French men are obsessed with the opposite sex. It was seen as something of a status symbol to have a couple of mistresses as well as a loving wife. Of course this takes a fair bit of 'energy' to keep everybody happy and Voronoff noticed that many older French men were becoming a bit 'lackluster' in the bedroom.

After 18 years of mulling over the problem the good doctor came up with the obvious solution – he would take slices of testicles from young virile apes and transplant them into the scrotums of middle aged men.

This monkey is in the mood for lovin'!

Now if you a squirm a bit while you read this, that is fine – it has squirm-factor 1,000 I reckon. Voronoff would lie an ape or monkey on an operating table next to the human patient. Both would be knocked out and have their scrotums cut open. He then extracted the monkey testicle and cut it into six slices. Then he used something like a cheese grater to roughen up the side of the testicle strip and did the same to the exposed human testicle. Finally, he taped the two together and sewed the whole lot up! Yowser x 1,000!!!

The idea was that the healthy, young monkey testicle would take over and re-invigorate the old human testicle. Believe it or not, in many cases, the men who had the operation reported fantastic results. The Doctor even put out a book saying what a great procedure it was and the book included before and after shots. The 'before' shot showed some gloomy old bugger with drooping grey whiskers and big old bags under his eyes. The 'after' shot showed the same person who had been morphed into a cheerful young fellow with bristling whiskers, red cheeks and a lusty look in his eye.

Monkey testicle grafting had some unfortunate side effects.

Of course the book didn't have any pictures of the poor monkeys who had been de-knackered.

CRAZY CURES

This is one of the first examples of the 'placebo'# effect. A placebo is when the patient is given a 'cure' such as a sugar pill which has no medical benefit. But the 'placebo' makes the patient think they are getting treatment so they begin to feel better. If the patient was lucky enough to recover, and some didn't, their body naturally absorbed the foreign flesh over a period of time.

Nevertheless, the procedure was such as success that Voronoff made a fortune and traveled the world selling his 'xenotransplants'. Other surgeons took up the procedure and thousands of patients were treated all over the world from America to India and even into Russia. Some men were so impressed with the results that they came back for a second helping! More money than sense obviously.

By the 1940s it was proved that in fact the body just broke down the implant and the procedure began to die out. But Voronoff obviously had something going on as he married a woman 25 years his junior and had several mistresses at the same time.

WARNING – WARNING – GROSS OUT ALERT
USING HUMANS TO CURE HUMANS

In ancient and medieval times there were a lot of humans around. Living or dead, their bits and pieces were seen as good medicine.

As far back as the Romans, human body parts were seen as good for medicine. The Romans loved their gladiators and saw them as strong and vital. They thought that if they ate parts of those gladiators the vitality would spread to them and cure their ills. No doubt you've seen lots of pictures of gladiators fighting each other and looking up at the emperor to get the thumbs up or thumbs down signal. What these pictures don't show are the sick Roman patients waiting at the side of the arena for a fix of ***FRESH GLADIATOR BLOOD***.

Pliny the Elder wrote that while a gladiator gasped out his last breath epileptics would leap onto his body and gulp down as much of his blood as they could. After the body was carted away surgeons would cut out the liver. Their patients were advised to eat one piece with breakfast for nine days as a cure of epilepsy.

CRAZY CURES

'Hurry up and die.'

These cures are pretty much based on superstition mixed with magic and medicine. There were so many bodies around that it was natural that they would be used for medicinal healing. An example of the mix between medicine and magic can be seen in this charm; an infatuated lover was advised to soak small pieces of bread in a gladiator's blood before casting them onto soil. He was then to throw a handful of the soil inside the house of his heart's desire before going to sleep. When he awoke in the morning he would find that the young lady returned his affections.

FASCINATING FACT
THE NOSES HAVE IT

Sometimes I look at noses. I wonder why some people have tiny little flat noses while others have big honkers with LOTS of nasal hair sticking out in clumps that look like spider legs. How do you feel about your nose, is it too small, too big or just right?
Well whatever you feel about your nose (mine is okay, although it gets a bit sniffly at times) you've got thousands of generations of ancestors to thank for it.

Arthur Thompson was a Victorian anthropologist and he noticed that people of African descent have shorter noses with wider nostrils while people from colder climates like Northern Europe have longer thinner noses. Being called Mr. Thompson, Arthur called this 'Thompson's rule'.

Recent studies have found that Thompson was right on the money. The size of peoples' noses is directly related to where they live on the globe. And noses have a very important function. People in a warm moist environment have small noses with wider nostrils since the air is nice and warm when it enters the lungs it is at the right temperature. Also, the mucus on the nasal hairs is nice and moist, ensuring that bacteria and virus are caught on their sticky surfaces before getting to the lungs and causing troubles.

People in colder, drier climates need a super nose – it has to be longer so that as air is drawn in it is warmed up, they also need more nose hairs since they are less moist and can catch less bugs or nasties! (Scientists think that Neanderthals had huge noses. Since they lived near the arctic circle hunting mammoths they needed a huge hooter to warm up the air.)

All we need now is a scientist to do a booger count – which kind of nose would produce more boogers do you think?

GROSS MEDICINE

The Middle Ages were pretty sexist. Men owned their wives and daughters and could treat them pretty much how they wanted. Women could not inherit property and young families would try to marry off their daughters as soon as possible.

If that wasn't bad enough, boy's urine was seen as a much better medicine than girl's urine. One recipe to cure indigestion called for the urine of a twelve-year-old boy (Why a twelve-year-old? I have no idea.) to be put in a glass jar and left to ferment for several months. The vile concoction was then mixed with herbs and the poor patient would have to gulp down a spoonful every morning. The Apothecary# who wrote this recipe said it was very successful and he never had patients coming back for more! No wonder. One dose would be enough for me.

In the West Highlands of Scotland, it was advised to dry and powder human excrement and blow it in the eye to cure blindness. The dung of an infant was seen as particularly effective. Distilled oil from the faeces of children was an effective cure for dandruff when applied to the scalp. Distillation is a smelly business at best, but distilling faeces must have been a particularly horrible activity. The same oil taken orally was considered a sure-fire cure for cancer in 13th Century France. If urine was 'stale and rank' it could be drunk to cure pleurisy, fever and asthma, while constipation was tackled by a stiff draught of one's own urine every morning followed by one or two hours of fasting.

Barbequed dog turd strapped to a wound was recommended by the Countess of Kent, while distilled horse, chicken oxen and pig poo was a cure for pleurisy. A jaundiced patient could be cured if he urinated on warm steaming horse dung. Peacock dung cured vertigo (dizziness). Rat droppings, 5 a day, were a cure for constipation. A balding fellow who wanted to make himself more appealing to the opposite sex was advised to mix rat droppings with honey and onion and smear the stuff onto his scalp to make the hair grow back and impress the ladies!

To be honest I'd prefer to stay single!

Human waste was also used in cosmetics. Women in Ancient Rome smeared poo over their faces to preserve a youthful complexion.

Restoration women washed their faces in their own urine to keep them fresh. Ashes of goat's dung mixed with oil stopped them losing their hair. A sure fire way to clear the pores was to wash your face with honey, vinegar, milk and a boy's urine all mixed up together.

CORPSE CURES

The belief that fresh blood could cure 'epilepsy' survived beyond Roman times. While we know that epilepsy is caused by scrambled electronic signals in the brain, in the Middle Ages lots of ailments were placed under this umbrella term. It was known as 'the falling sickness'. Strokes, heart attacks, fainting fits and all manner of horrible things were lumped in with this illness. As a result, lots of cures were needed for this common problem.

The best place to get fresh human blood was to attend executions. Throughout Germany and France, the most common means of executing people was by chopping off their heads with swords. The 'Headsmen' were quite well paid for their work, but they were able to pick up a bit of extra cash by selling fresh blood. He often had a couple of cups standing ready and, as soon as the offending head was lopped off, the Headsman would collect some good doses of blood and hand it to the waiting customers.

Once they had had a good dose of blood the patients would run off as quickly as possible. Why, you may ask? Guilt? Remorse? None of these. It was accepted wisdom that by running off you would spread the blood's vitality through your body so it would do the most good. Believe it or not this practice continued in Germany right up to 1845.

Executioners could make money other ways too. People believed that by touching a hanged man's hand against their chest or cheeks they could be cured of eczema, piles and gout. Young children held against a fresh corpse would be cured of all ailments and a peace of hangman's rope rubbed against a tooth cured tooth decay!

The corpses did not necessarily have to be fresh. In London, the main apothecaries' district was situated near Bucklersbury, just down from St Pancreas. The city's most notorious criminals were gibbeted in this area and many apothecaries took their clients to touch the suspended cadavers. This was said to cure cancer and goiter.

As you can see, all of this is pretty horrible and superstitious nonsense, but it does prove one thing – people would do absolutely anything to get better. Just like we would today, really.

Just to finish this chapter on a positive note. I did read one cure which was to stop nosebleeds by stuffing moss up your nostrils. This would actually work as many mosses have naturally occurring disinfectant chemicals in them, so they could actually cure somebody. However, another doctor recommended stuffing warm pig poo mixed with chalk up your nostrils. I know which I'd prefer.

Who needs tissues when you've got pig poo?

EUNUCHS

Most operations are made to heal sick people. But there was one operation that was very common in China up until the early 20th Century which was done on perfectly healthy young men – Castration#. The boys who had this operation were called 'Eunuchs'.

Now, don't read on if you're a sensitive young fellow who doesn't like gory bits.

Eunuchs were very valuable in Chinese society. They were seen as trusted servants who would not try and steal their master's assets (since they couldn't give them to their children) and would not try to have sex with their master's wife (since they couldn't).

At one stage there were 10,000 eunuchs in the Chinese Imperial Palace that we now call the 'Forbidden city'. The idea was that, even though there could be lots of men in the palace, there would only be one 'real' man. This was the Emperor who still had all of his 'bits and pieces'. The Emperor could have several hundred wives. Of course not all of these wives could see their husband regularly so the eunuchs were there to keep them out of trouble. In fact, the most important eunuch was the one who determined which wife would get to 'meet up' with the Emperor at night time.

Now I'm sure the question you want to ask is – how did a eunuch become a eunuch? Believe it or not many families volunteered their sons to become one. At the time many Chinese were desperately poor, so it was seen as a great career move to get family members working in the Imperial Palace or for a rich noble. Having a eunuch or two was seen as a great status symbol. So rather than having a Porsche or a private jet, rich people would boast about their eunuchs!

Once a young lad had been volunteered he was taken to an area just outside the Imperial Palace. This was where the professional castrators had their shops. Only a select few families had permission to carry out this operation and they had to have a licence from the emperor. Many families had been in the business for hundreds of years (I'd prefer to be a carpenter to be honest).

These families were known as 'knifers' and their first duty was to ask the volunteer to recline on a low bed. By law, they had to ask if the patient would regret being castrated. They could only proceed if he said "no regrets" (I'd run a mile at this stage). They then wrapped his legs with bandages and gave him some opium laced tea. They cleaned the genitals with schezuan pepper and the knifer grabbed the whole lot and whipped them off with a razor sharp blade!

Yowser!!!

They then placed a metal plug where the penis used to be; after 3 days this was removed. If the young fellow could wee the operation was deemed a success. If he couldn't wee the poor man would be in for a painful death.

These 'knifers' were real professionals and most (98%) of their subjects survived this process and went on to become happy little eunuchs. This is quite remarkable as, before modern anaesthetics and disinfectants, most people died from surgery.

Actually, being a eunuch had some health benefits. They lived up to twenty years longer than their brothers and had much less heart disease. There were some down sides though for sure. Chief among them was incontinence# which got worse as they got older. They had to wear man sized nappies and there was a common Chinese saying "as smelly as a eunuch".

FASCINATING FACTS
CHINESE SUPERSTITION AND EUNUCHS

For thousands of years the Chinese have believed that to get to a happy afterlife your whole body has to buried in one piece. This made it very difficult for eunuchs.

A eunuch is a person who has had his testicles removed either as a punishment or so he can become an attendant to the Chinese Emperor! Most were given this 'surgery' when they were young. Their testicles and penis were then placed in a little jar and the eunuch had to carry them around with him until he died, then they would be placed in his coffin with his corpse before being buried.

But, of course, some eunuchs lost their 'little package'. So they would steal some other poor fellow's bits and carry them to the grave. Obviously it didn't matter that it was your whole body that was buried as long as it had all the requisite parts!

Chinese are pretty concerned with this as if you don't enter the happy afterlife with a proper burial you come back as a ghost. And there are no happy Chinese ghosts it seems. They are all miserable and angry and always try to take out this anger on the living.

Eunuch grave.

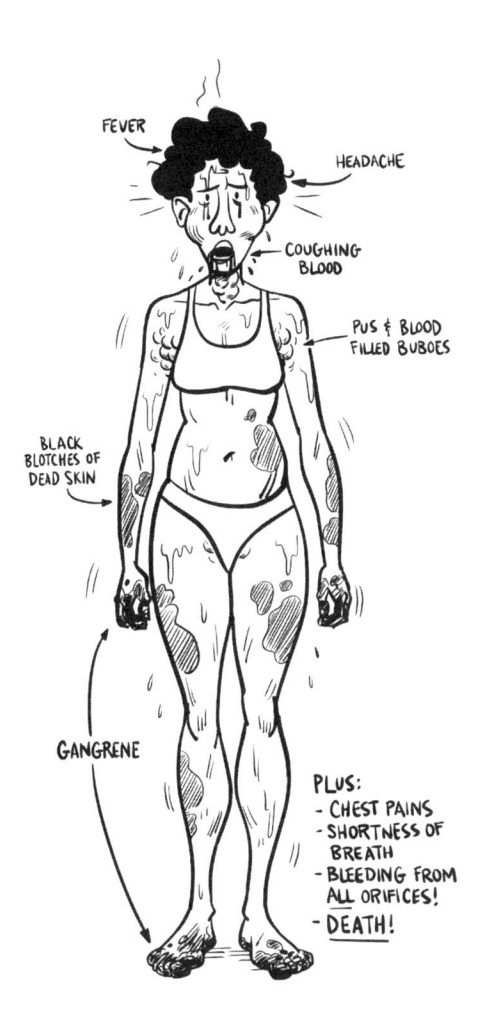

CHAPTER 8

THE BLACK DEATH

The barmy bacteria strikes

There were hundreds of 'cures' for the Black Death. These usually involved eating and drinking horrific medicines or strapping decomposing animals onto your legs etc. Little did the sufferers of the plague realise that all of their ills were spread by a mad-psycho-killer flea!

It was thought that the Black Death or plague was caused by Miasma. In order to clear the air, children were told to smoke as much tobacco as possible. Another suspected source of Miasma was cat and dog fur so as soon as the plague arrived every poor little moggy or pooch was hunted down and dispatched. This let the rats breed unchecked which meant more and more mad-psycho-killer fleas. But more on them later.

Smoking can be good for your health – it frightens off fleas.

Nowadays a lot of people get rich selling vitamins, which basically gives us the most expensive urine in the world.

Doctor Peter Lillicrap had a similar scam when he sold a book in 1665 entitled Seven and fifty approved recipes against the plague. He sold a lot of books but probably didn't do one iota of good for any of his readers.

Here are some of his favourite recipes (Lillicrap had a speech impediment. Can you work out what it was?):

Take and onion and cut it into four pieces. Cut a piece out of each qwuater and fill it with tweacle. Wap the wejoined onion in white linen and woast it in some coals. Once it is cooked squeeze out the juices and give the patient a spoonful and soon he would feel a whole lot better.

Gwind some dwied seeds from a bay tree and mix it with a little salt. As soon as the patient feels a fever he should mix this with some water and vinegar and have a good lie down covewed with sheep skins. If symptoms persist, use wine instead of vinegar.

Fill a glass one third full of tweacle, one third full of spwing water and one third full of the urine of a young boy virgin who exhibits good health. Dwink this thwee days in a row. The Venetians swear by this cure.

The patient should dwink good quality tweacle and eat chestnuts. Then wub tweacle on the buboes, cut a pigeon in half and lie the pigeon halves with the feather outwards on the gwowths. Once the pigeon flesh turns gween it should be wemoved and squeezed. Any gween juices that emerge from the pigeon have been sucked from the bubo.

Take the oldest oil you can get and boil it for sevewal hours. Once this has been done put 50 scorpions per pound of oil into the mixture and cook it until it has weduced by a third. Once this has been done pull out the scworpions and stwain the mixture thwough some cloth into another container and leave this in the sun for thwee months or in the ashes of a fire for four days. Once this has been done put in two ounces of Unicorn horn, one ounce of tweacle and some pure water. Once a patient starts to feel bad, appwy this lotion to the chest above the heart, the neck and the wwists there will be a marvewous effect.

Pluck the feathers fwom the bottom of a chicken where the 'egge doth emerge' and hold the beast against the buboes so that it can absorb all of the pestilence within.

I'm not sure what the chicken would think about having its bum plucked and held against a puss filled buboes but I sure wouldn't be happy about it!

Medieval Medicine – the chicken bum plague sponge!

PSYCHO FLEA

As you have seen, all different kinds of bacteria and viruses have different survival strategies to make sure they can do the maximum amount of damage, or make sure that we spread them around like confetti at a wedding. The Plague bacteria Yersinia pestis is like a diabolical evil genius from a James Bond movie in the way it manipulates all kinds of animals and insects.

"Yes Mr Bond – all I want is world domination – mwhah ha ha."

108   THE BLACK DEATH

But unlike most villains whose murderous plots are stopped by the good guys, this bacterium has successfully killed millions upon millions of people and even toppled some civilizations.

Yersinia pestis is named after the Swiss scientist who first discovered the rod shaped bacteria. His name was Alexander Yersin. I'm not sure that I'd want a bacterium that has killed millions of people after me, but obviously doctor Yersin was not that fussed.

Anyway, this bacterium is the most nasty, conniving and tricky bug you would ever want to meet.

It is endemic# to several parts of Asia and America and lives harmlessly in the guts of small mammals such as prairie dogs or rats. Sometimes it enters into the carrier's blood stream and then embarks on its campaign of mass murder.

It waits in the steadily sickening host's circulatory system until a poor luckless flea comes along. The flea is merely minding its own business and looking for a snack, but it gets a lot more than it bargained for. Once the insect sucks up the blood, the bacteria makes the blood clot in the flea's belly rather than moving into the digestive system. This tricks the flea into thinking it is ravenously thirsty and hungry.

The poor bloodsucker goes crazy and leaps onto anything it can sense that is warm and has a pulse. Fleas don't have wings but their legs act like springs and allow them to leap distances 50 times their own body length. It sinks its proboscis into the new animal's skin and does a tiny flea sized vomit. But, in this vomit are thousands of Plague bacteria. The flea sucks in what it can, but of course, its guts are still blocked so it is still hungry and leaps onto another animal and the whole ghastly process is repeated.

I don't like fleas but even you must admit it is easy to feel sorry for the little creature. Its guts were filled up with what must be a massive case of indigestion and no food is being digested, so it begins to starve to death. But the Yersinia pestis pulls another trick out of its amazing survival strategies. Just as the flea is about to expire from hunger and exhaustion the bacteria lets the blood meal through to the guts to give nutrition.

Watch out for fleas with tummy upsets – they can turn deadly!

The flea recovers its strength almost immediately. After having a little rest it begins to feel hungry again and, you guessed it, the whole process starts over. The flea jumps around onto as many people as possible sucking their blood and infecting them with the Bubonic Plague.

The Plague bacterium rubs it plague hands with glee – the entrée has been successfully consumed – now for the main course.

THREE TYPES OF PLAGUE

The Plague is not a lottery you want to win.

110   THE BLACK DEATH

Many diseases, such as TB, have different ways of attacking the body. Well the Plague is no different. It's no wonder that people who were attacked by the Plague thought that God/Gods/Supreme deity were angry with them. The symptoms seemed to get worse and worse and worse (and worse) as the disease took hold.

BUBONIC PLAGUE

This is often called 'the benign plague' because it's not as bad as its relatives. How something that caused 70% death rate of infected people in four of five days after infection can be called benign is beyond me. This version had the bacteria spreading into the lymphatic system# and setting up shop in the lymph glands. The first sign were small lumps found in the throat, under the arms and within the groin (yowser!). These harmless little lumps soon became horrific balls of white hot pain known as 'buboes'.

These golf ball sized pustules of pain are filled with pus, blood and decomposed fleshbloodpain. Situated where they are, any attempt to move sends shooting pains up and down the entire body. The bacteria live under the skin and kills millions of cells leading to large black blotches of dead skin which gave the disease its other name – the Black Death. Eventually the bacteria get into organs and overwhelm the immune system. Things get so bad that gangrene begins to rot the hands and feet. Even the central nervous system, which controls speech and actions, is attacked so that the poor old victim staggers around in a funny jerking way raving crazily like a pus infected loon!

Oh, and the smell. Rotting flesh, lungs and underarms meant that the sufferers stank to high heaven. Not Nice.

The good news – 30% survived this disease, built up resistance and had kids who inherited the resistance. This led to fewer deaths in the future.

PNEUMONIC PLAGUE

The 'Benign' plague sounds pretty 'unbenign' to me, but even worse was the 'Pneumonic plague'. Rather than setting up shop in the lymphatic system, the bacteria found its way into some poor soul's lungs. They began to cough and sprayed a deadly package into the lungs of all their friends and loved ones who got sick too.

The initial symptoms are, of course, coughing, which degenerates into coughing blood. This is followed by fever, headache, shortness of breath, chest pains and watery sputum (spit). The entire respiratory system shuts down as it is overwhelmed with fluids that can't be expelled from the lungs and heart failure follows.

99% of patients died within 36 hours, gasping out their life and no doubt using their last breath to pray for mercy!

When this disease went through whole towns it's easy to see how you could almost imagine a huge skeleton armed with a scythe mowing down countless innocent people.

Lots of people are reported fleeing their wives, husbands or even children as soon as they got sick. No wonder.

> **DID YOU KNOW (You probably did, everybody knows this)**
> Pneumonic Plague is the subject of the common child's nursery rhyme 'Ring a ring of Roses'.
> 'Ring a ring of roses' refers to blotches on the skin – one of the first symptoms.
> The 'pocket full of posies' represents the bunches of aromatics that people would hold under their noses to try and avoid sickness (herb prices skyrocketed during outbreaks). 'A tishoo, a tishoo' of course represents the coughing and sneezing, and 'we all fall down' is pretty self-explanatory.

SEPTICAEMIC PLAGUE

This type makes the other two look pretty good. The bacteria are injected straight into the bloodstream where it begins breeding furiously. The white blood cells try to fight back, but to no avail, and soon all of the poor person's blood starts clotting everywhere. This means that oxygen is not taken into the limbs and skin and soon fingers, toes, nose, ears, and pretty much everything else begins to die! Cell walls begin to break down and soon the patient begins to bleed out of their mouth, eyes, nose and even rectum (bum). Pretty much

100% of people died within 3 or 4 hours of contracting this type. But during this time their blood was so filled with bacteria that any flea that bit into him would guarantee survival of the 'Bubonic Plague'.

ORIGIN OF THE MEDIEVAL PLAGUE

Bill Boghurst (yes that is his real name) wrote about signs that the plague was approaching hundreds of years ago. These included: changing weather, war, children playing dead, animals dying, cloudy weather without rain, cold nights and hot days. He also told people to look out for the following human behaviour that meant the plague was coming: feeling cold, stiff neck, staring, idle chat, sighing, sitting, anxiety or headaches. Considering that these things happen all the time anyway poor doctor Boghurst must have been in a perpetual state of fear.

What the medieval people didn't know was that the disease was carried in fleas. What they did know, after the first 'great dying' in the 1340s, was that the plague came back every 10 years or so. No wonder Bill was worried. But that was later on. The first big attack of killer plague came at the beginning of the 14th Century.

In a remote corner of China, in about 1318 CE a little rodent was not feeling too well. While all of its relatives were having a great old time eating grass and sniffing each other's bottoms, this little character had a splitting headache. He had also lost his appetite, something which rodents NEVER do. A hunter came across the little, four-legged clan. While most bolted underground, our sick little friend was too weak and was snatched up by the hunter. He popped the sick animal into his bag and preceded homewards to cook it up in a stir fry.

But he didn't only bring home something to eat, he also bought home a deadly infection. When the rodent died a flea leapt off its old host onto the human. It bit into the human and what took place is called a 'cross species transfer'.

Rats traveled around the world in cargoes of cloth – they bought a nasty surprise.

Several thousand Yersinia pestis were transferred into a human host and the deadliest outbreak of the plague in the history of mankind began – all thanks to one little rodent who should have stayed in bed!

The Chinese peasant who had caught the rodent probably already had quite a lot on his plate. In the years before 1318 China had been hit by a huge array of natural disasters. There had been floods, famines and earthquakes. Locusts had decimated lots of crops and millions had died from these assorted calamities.

But they were nothing compared to what was about to hit them. The Plague began near the Chinese border with Myanmar and soon ravaged China. So many died that the Yuan dynasty was bought to the brink of collapse.

Joining China and Europe was the Silk Road. This wasn't named because it was made of silk, rather because Chinese traders carried silk and lots of other luxury goods directly into the heart of Europe. Fleas must have hitched a ride in this silk and by 1346 a Mongol army on the Black Sea was infected.

Mongols were some of the fiercest warriors ever, In 1346 the Mongol army of the 'Khanate of The Golden Horde' were busy besieging the town of Caffa. At the time Caffa was owned by Italians from the town of Genoa.

When the plague hit the Mongolian soldiers they did the only thing that fierce warriors could have done. Rather than burying their dead in a respectful manner, they loaded the flea infested corpses onto catapults and lobbed them over the walls of Caffa onto the Italian defenders. This had the desired effect and soon the Italians were dying in droves. The town's populations hauled all of the corpses down to the dockyards and threw them into the sea but it was not enough and they decided to flee (not flea). They loaded their survivors onto a few galleys and rowed through the Black sea into the Mediterranean and back home to Italy.

"Incoming!!!" Medieval germ warfare.

When Yellow Fever (see chapter on mosquitoes) was ravaging parts of America, some bright sparks came up with the idea of inspecting ships before they landed. If any of the crew or passengers were sick then the ship had to stay offshore for 30 days after any symptoms had stopped. This was called 'quarantine' and is still used today.

But 700 years ago there was no such thing and the galleys stopped at several places on the way back to Italy. They were the original 'plague ships' and left the Black Death at Constantinople and Sicily where it began to ravage the population. By the time the galleys got to Italy only a few survivors staggered ashore, accompanied by a horde of rats.

At the time Europe was having something of a population boom and the brown rat (which is an excellent climber), and its deadly cargo of Yersinia pestis, was let onto an unsuspecting population like a fox in a henhouse (if foxes get into chicken coop they don't only kill what they need to eat but kill every bird in there).

By the end of 1347 the Plague had engulfed Corsica and Sardinia and reached Marseille in France. By mid-1348 most of France and Spain was infected and by December 1349 England and the German states had experienced the full horror of the deadly disease. Egypt was struck in 1347, and soon it covered the Arabian Peninsula.

Europe lost at least half of its population. North Africa and the Islamic states of the East lost between one third to half of its people as did India. The original source of the plague, China, saw its population drop from 120 million to approximately 65 million.

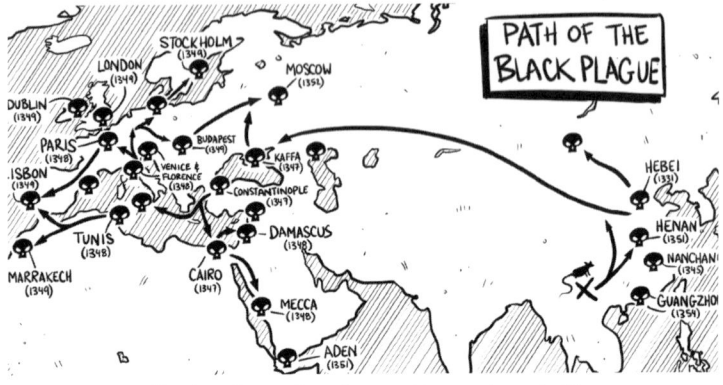

Death on the march – where would you go to escape it?

CATASTROPHE

Next time you are at the shops or sitting in a school assembly imagine what it would be like if two thirds of the people sitting around you were to suddenly die! While it might not be too bad seeing the end of Mrs Smythe your French teacher, it would be pretty sad seeing all of your friends and family knocked off. The Plague had hit Europe in the 5th Century BCE and the 6th Century CE, as well as 'The Great Dying' when it hit in the 1340s. Each time it seemed that society itself was about to collapse.

CATASTROPHE QUIZ D.O.T.D.

DISPOSAL OF THE DEAD

I know it sounds awful but one of the biggest problems was what to do with all of the dead people who were killed by the Plague. I'm sure you've had the experience of opening the fridge door and finding it a bit whiffy. If you find a suspect sausage or a harmful ham it's straight into the bin with it.

But when the plague went through a town half of the population often died, if not more. This meant tons and tons of people had to be disposed of, somehow. Some of the methods used were pretty gruesome so skip to the next chapter if you have a sensitive tummy.

(Answers at the bottom of p. 118)

WHICH OF THESE METHODS WERE USED TO DISPOSE OF THE DEAD? (Tick the box)

- ❏ Place them on barges and dump them out at sea
- ❏ Cover them with rocks so dogs could not dig them up
- ❏ Dig huge pits called corpse pits and toss them all in
- ❏ Do a 'lasagna' burial – between each row of corpses put a layer of dirt.
- ❏ Chuck them in a river (consecrate the river first)
- ❏ Put them out the front door and wait for them to be collected
- ❏ Leave them in their houses but board up the windows and doors
- ❏ Wait until you see a priest with a funeral procession and join in with your dead relative to get free funeral

---

WHICH OF THESE METHODS WAS USED TO PREVENT INFECTIONS? (Tick the boxes)

- ❏ Throw yourself in a cistern
- ❏ Run away to the country side
- ❏ Abandon your relatives as soon as they get sick
- ❏ Live in a big cage and only let things be passed to you with a stick

- ❐ Live in the middle of an orchard or vineyard
- ❐ Burn the clothes of those who were infected
- ❐ Light huge fires indoors burning herbs
- ❐ Smoke tobacco
- ❐ Bury mothers and their dead children at crossroads posed like Maddona and Baby Jesus
- ❐ Kill all cats and dogs so they don't spread the miasma
- ❐ Live a pure life and don't get drunk
- ❐ Get drunk and carry on in pubs
- ❐ Avoid lust, pride, swearing, profit, plaesure, feasting, theatre, hypocrisy, greed, lack of charity, heresy, wine, beer, water, charms, jewellry, witchcraft, bathing, vomiting, swimming in rivers, vomiting and getting emotional (all these are from Doctor Boghurst)

WHICH OF THESE METHODS WAS USED TO SAY SORRY TO GOD? (Tick the boxes)

- ❐ Consult an oracle
- ❐ Pray to the holy Virgin Agatha of Catania
- ❐ Beat yourself with sticks and whips
- ❐ Attack all 'heretics' and kill them
- ❐ Pray

ANSWERS – Tick all the boxes – They are all true.

FASCINATING FACT
THE FLAGELLANTS

Everybody loves it when the traveling carnival comes to town. The Plague led to a new kind of carnival where 'The Flagellants' wandered through the country side beating themselves senseless. They used whips, planks, rods, hot irons and a whole lot of devilish things to thrash themselves until blood poured out of their backs. Some had whips with three tails, tied onto the end of each tail were nails or stones to add to the agony.

These religious folk thought that the Plague was god's way of punishing them, so if they punished themselves they would not have to be punished by god who would then get angry at somebody else and punish them instead!

Thousands would march in black cowls with their backs bare so that they could whip themselves. The leader would intone a prayer and, every now and again, the whole mass of people would throw themselves on the ground wailing and screaming and gnashing their teeth to show how sorry they were!

But this was not open to any joe-blow off the street. Only middle class people or wealthy peasants could join, and they had to pay a fair amount of money for the privilege of thrashing themselves. They also had to list all of the sins they had committed since the age of seven, as well as signing a pledge promising not to wash, drink, sleep in a bed or talk to a member of the opposite sex.

"Sorry sir — you're not rich enough for a good thrashing."

When they got to a town the flagellants went to the town square and formed a circle to begin their ceremony. Villagers would put sick people in the circle in the hope that they would be cured. Some even put dead Plague victims in there in the hope that they would be raised from the dead (presumably they were not too far gone and smelly).

Some of the members moved through the group, calling on Jesus to forgive their sins, while dirge like hymns were recited faster and faster. Several times they threw themselves to the ground writhing in sinful abasement to their god before they leapt up again and began thrashing themselves as the frenzy took hold. Each man or woman tried to outdo each other with the ferocity of their whipping and the earnestness of their entreaties. Beyond them the audience too entered a religious frenzy and howled and gibbered as a collective hysteria took over. Blood spattered the surrounding walls and crowds. Occasionally the barbs of the flails were embedded in the flesh and needed medical aid to extract them.

The flagellants became such a pest that some nobles banned them in their territory and had to arrest and torture the leaders to make them go away.

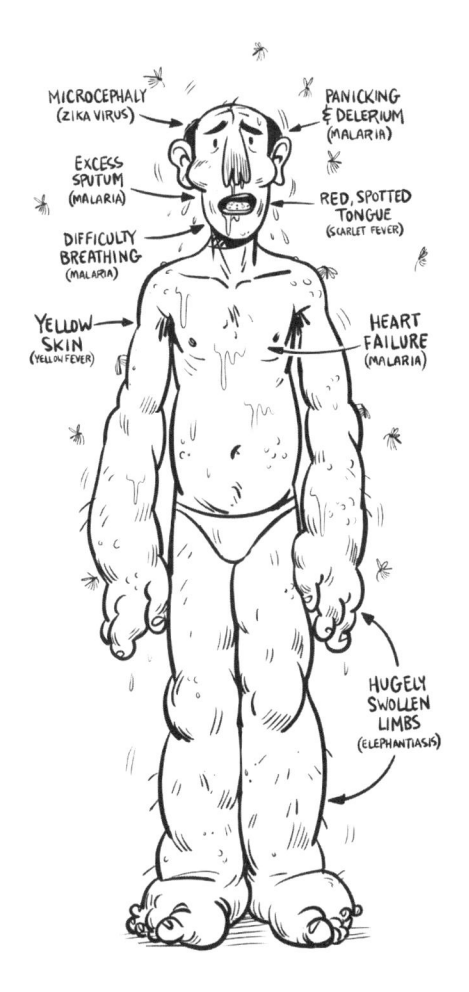

CHAPTER 9

BLOODSUCKERS AND MALARIA
*Things that go **bite** in the night*

Malaria is still one of the biggest killers in the world and every day thousands of people are infected by this deadly little parasite. For thousands of years humans have been knocked around by this disease, even when The Roman Empire was at its height there were large areas of swamp just near Rome that were uninhabitable due to 'swamp fever', as it was known.

It's not hard to see why. Once the tiny little parasite gets into the blood stream it jumps into red blood cells and has a party. The cell looks like any other cell but inside the parasite is breeding and eating up the cell contents until BANG the whole cell explodes and 32 brand new little malarias are released to attack another 32 human blood cells. In a matter of days, the host's bloodstream is awash with millions of terminator cells and lots of dead blood matter that gunks up the circulatory system, and that can lead to death.

But, while malaria has been effecting humans for thousands of years, it has been effecting mosquitoes for millions. Once the malaria gets into the blood sucking insect it turns it into a 'terminator' mosquito that has super sensitive scenting equipment that allows it to sniff out new victims from miles away.

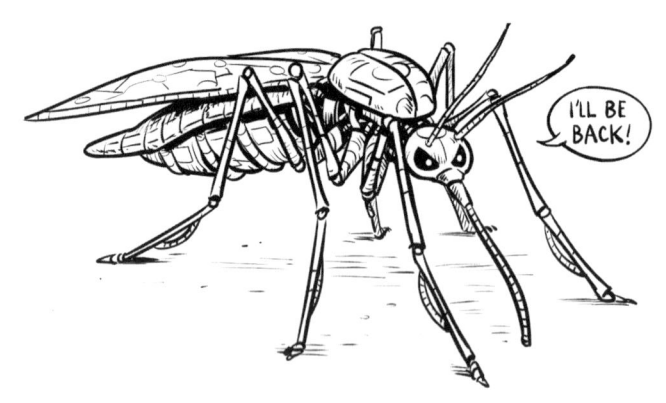

"If there's one thing I hate – it's a happy human!"

Malaria is only one of the many diseases that can be given to humans by your local mozzie, here are some of the most interesting and gross infections.

124   BLOODSUCKERS AND MALARIA

> **FACINATING FACTS**
> # MOSQUITOES
>
> Male mosquitoes only live for one or two weeks. Females live four times longer.
> The fastest mosquito travels at about 3 kilometres per hour.
> Males feed on nectar and plant juices. Females need to suck blood so they can provide proteins and iron for her eggs.
> 'Mosquito' is Spanish for 'little fly'.
> They are the deadliest animals on earth. They infect and kill more humans than any other critter.
> They make that irritating whining noise because their wings beat at 600 times a minute.
> Mosquitoes find us by following the carbon dioxide that we breathe out from up to 80 feet away.
> An average mosquito dinner is 5 millionths of a litre of blood.
> Some 79-million-year-old mosquitoes have been found preserved in Canadian amber. Some dated to 49 million years old still have blood in their belly.

ZIKA VIRUS

The amazing thing about mosquito borne diseases is that new ones pop up all of the time. Athletes going to the Rio de Janeiro games didn't only have to worry about muggers and bash artists, they had to beware of a previously unheard disease – the Zika virus.

Although it had first been found in 1947 in Africa, one of the first large outbreaks was in Rio, just before the 2016 Olympic games. The virus is carried in common mosquitoes and the symptoms are pretty mild to say the least. A mild rash, a bit of an itch and maybe a sniffle combined with a temperature; that's all that adults feel. These symptoms don't sound too bad do they? That's pretty much all an adult gets, but if the infected person is pregnant things are a whole lot worse.

About a hundred years ago a very popular type of entertainment was the 'Side Show'. These were also known as 'Freak Shows' and allowed paying members of the public to see all kinds of unfortunate individuals who had birth defects or were a bit different somehow. The 'Bearded Lady' or the 'Siamese Twins' were favourites back then. But any good side show worth its while had a couple of 'Pin Heads'.

Zip.

These unfortunate fellows had a full sized face but only a tiny pointed skull with a very small brain. The most famous performer was Zip the Pinhead who was with the Barnum and Bailey circus.

Back then people were pretty cruel and didn't hesitate to call people names, but we now refer to this condition as Macrophaly. For whatever reason Zika moves into the womb and infects the baby, preventing the brain from developing.

Zika is a pretty nasty disease, but if you're not pregnant it does not really pose a threat.

MALARIA

Malaria is caused by Protozoa that infect a victim's blood. These little single cell bugs have been around for millions of years and the first identified ones were found preserved in amber and are at least 30 million years old. It seems that the disease developed in Africa and over this huge amount of time learned how to infect all kinds of animals including birds, rodents and even reptiles. Some diseases are limited because not many insects carry them around, but Malaria is incredibly dangerous thanks to at least 65 kinds of mosquitoes that carry it around in their gut.

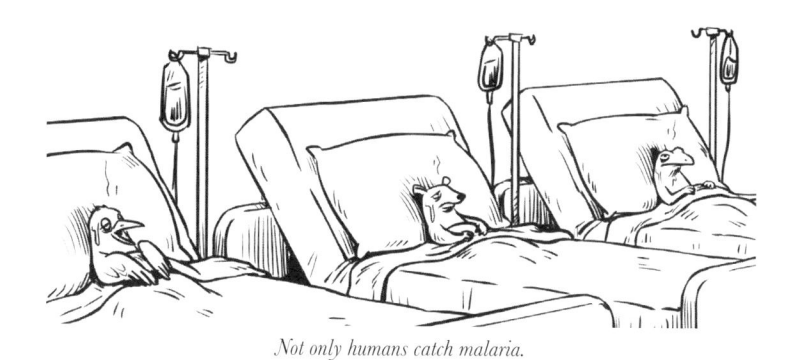

Not only humans catch malaria.

The name malaria comes from the Italian word 'mal aria' bad air. The miasmic theory comes from malaria as this theory said that people could get sick if they were infected by 'miasmas' which rose from smelly, still water. This kind of water is exactly where mosquitoes love to set up shop.

If you read really old books there are lots of references to funny sounding diseases. Malaria had lots and lots of names. These names included; Ague, Miasmic Fever, Jungle Fever, Congestive Fever, Remitting Fever, Bilious Fever, Paludal Poison, Swamp Sickness, The Shakes, Malignant Fever, Benin Blight and Swamp Fever.

The reason that doctors gave the same disease so many names is because there are so many symptoms that can be created by Malaria that they did not know they were dealing with the same thing. The little protozoan parasites are incredibly clever and come out to attack the host's body, feeding off blood cells and having a bit of party, but then they disappear and hide in the liver before coming out and living it up again.

There are four kinds of malaria and each one produces different symptoms. Plasmodium falciparum, Plasmodium vivax, Plasmodium ovale and Plasmodium malariae are all carried around in the guts of trillions of mosquitoes. If a mosquito is not infected but bites an infected human, it picks up the infection, ready to pass it on to others.

When bitten by an infected mosquito, the patient begins to feel a slow rising of temperature. This then transforms into feverish heat interspersed by dreadful cold chills. One minute the patient is freezing cold with their teeth chattering like a wind up monkey head. Next minute they are pouring sweat and burning up like they've just eaten a particularly fiery Madras curry! Often they become delirious and rave on about nothing while turning yellow from anemia. These symptoms are caused as the malaria infect the patient's blood cells, cause them to burst and move onto fresh victims. Then, without rhyme or reason, the symptoms stop. Once they have had their fun the parasites pull their heads in and hibernate in the sufferer's liver until their next attack.

I'm sure you don't want to be infected but if you had a choice it's best to pick the P. vivax and P. ovale strains. Once these get into your system the little protozoa can hide inside your body for years and years. Occasionally they'll pop out and give you an attack of the shakes but then disappear for years and years.

P.falciparum is the real bad boy in the malaria family and you would not want to touch it with a barge pole.

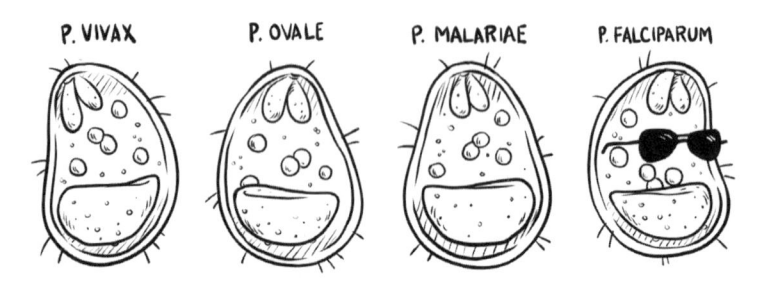

Don't take 'Bad Boy Falciparum' home to meet your parents.

BLOODSUCKERS AND MALARIA

Falciparum is like a rude uncle who does not know when to stop carrying on and partying. Like most people who don't know when to stop partying, they ruin everybody's fun and trash the premises. This is true of Falciparum. The protozoa attack so many red blood cells that there are not enough left to carry oxygen from the lungs around the body – this leads to the patient breathing furiously but not being able to get enough oxygen to the organs: the kidney, liver and spleen (whatever that is) begin to shut down. What's more, since there are so few blood cells, any little injury doesn't clot, and you bleed uncontrollably.

Then things get worse – the patient feels desperately panicky, no matter hard how they breathe they feel as if they are suffocating or drowning – this leads to chest pains as the heart desperately tries to pump more and more and more blood. The patient can't lie down since frothy 'sputum' (snot and saliva mixed up together) begins to fill up the lungs.

Death often arrives as the poor patient's heart gives up.

It seems that this malaria is a gift from our Gorilla cousins and it first evolved in their populations millions of years ago.

While reading this book you'll feel pretty chuffed because a lot of the diseases have been knocked on the head and aren't such a threat nowadays. Malaria isn't like that and at least half a billion people are still suffering from it. Malaria has been around for hundreds of thousands of years interacting with animals, but it wasn't until humans settled down as farmers that this dreadful disease really got its hooks in. Farmers need water. Mosquitoes need water. Malaria needs mosquitoes. Over the years malaria has managed to hitch a ride in hundreds of types of mosquitoes. This makes it almost impossible to eradicate. Kill one type of mosquito and another takes its place.

Malaria had been around for a long time and the little critters know how to get the best of us. The Chinese wrote about the symptoms in 2700 BCE and the Ancient Egyptians gave their workers unlimited amounts of garlic to try and keep the mozzies away.

Garlic breath of the Gods.

Mosquito nets were used by the richer ancient people. Hippocrates of Greece was no doubt a bright fellow but he was the first one to identify 'miasma' as the cause of malaria in the 4th century BCE. He thought it was foul gasses coming from swamps that caused the illness. No doubt he wrote about it at the same time as he was squashing mosquitoes.

A British army doctor found the cause of Malaria. While he was based in India, Ronald rRoss dissected hundreds of mosquitoes. He examined their belly contents and found the parasite in the belly of one that had recently sucked the blood of a malaria patient. He was the first to discover the link between the little bloodsuckers and the disease they spread.

YELLOW FEVER

In the 18th Century, Europeans and Americans were struck with a devastating new disease that seemed to come from nowhere. It turned the poor, awestruck people yellow as they became horribly feverish and demented. The most frightening thing about this disease was the final symptom. Although the patient would act like a raving loony for a week or two, just before they died they would suddenly become rational and sane. Some patients thought that maybe they had beaten the disease. Others knew they were having their last moments on this earth.

FANTASTIC FACT
SCARLET FEVER

Scarlet Fever is not at all related to yellow fever and gets its name from the patient's tongue, which turns Strawberry red and has little spots just like the fruit's skin.

"I'd prefer blueberries."

In the 20th Century it was one of the main killers of young people from 5 to 15 years old. It is caused by a bacteria and other symptoms include: a sore throat, fever, hallucinations and red rash like measles. Penicillin is an effective cure now, but the first cure called the 'Dick Test' was developed by Mr. and Mrs. Dick in 1924 (Gladys Henry Dick and George Frederick Dick)!

Over time people and animals develop a 'resistance' to disease. If a population is hit with a new disease a certain number will die. Others will not get infected and some will get infected and survive. The survivors hand their genes down to the next generation which then has a greater 'resistance' to the disease.

When a disease hits a new population it does the greatest damage. Such was the case of Yellow Fever. When Europeans started bringing slaves from Africa to America they also brought Yellow Fever. The Africans had resistance, as they had lived with if for thousands of years. The Europeans were not so lucky.

Monkeys living in the rainforest of West Africa were the original carriers of the Yellow Fever virus. When they were hunted and eaten the virus entered into humans. It is a 'hemorrhagic virus' similar to Ebola and leads to internal bleeding. Since the kidneys and liver aren't functioning the patient gets jaundice and turns yellow. The Spanish had another name for it 'The Black Vomit Disease'. It was called this because that was another symptom. The patient bled into his belly turning the vomit black. Yuck!!!

What was most frightening about Yellow Fever?

It would disappear for years and whole generations could go by without and infection. Then all of a sudden one little infected mosquito would bite one person. The virus filled up his blood and other mosquitoes would then pass it on until hundreds or thousands were dropping dead in the streets. Whole towns in the Americas and even Europe would be decimated.

Thankfully, when it was worked out that mosquitoes carried the disease, anybody with the symptoms was put in bed under a mosquito net so that he couldn't be used as an infectious blood bank for those pesky mossies.

By the way, not all mosquitoes are bad. Only the females suck blood. They have to do it to get energy to lay eggs that then turn into wrigglers.

By 1905 Yellow Fever had been pretty much contained so you don't have to worry about it.

FACINATING FACT
DENGUE FEVER

Dengue Fever is another virus from Africa. It isn't as deadly as Yellow Fever but infects the blood in a similar way. It is also known as 'Break Bone Fever' because one of the main symptoms is really, really agonising pain in the limbs that feels like your bones are broken! Africans thought it was the result of an evil spirit entering the patient's body. The pain is particularly severe in the head, back and limbs which pretty much covers everything!

Dengue Fever is making a comeback. It's been adopted by the most aggressive mosquito of all – The Asian Tiger Mosquito. This is the scariest mosquito ever. Unlike most of its cousins it swarms during the day and attacks people. In lots of places in Asia, if you head out for a picnic all you get is a mass of itchy bites as you're chased out of a park! Like all mosquito bites they stop itching after an hour. But if you are bitten by one hundred at once it is going to be a pretty unpleasant hour-worse than a period studying Geography!

The Asian Tiger Mosquito is more aggressive than a bucket full of blowflies.

ELEPHANTIASIS

There's a good chance that you have never heard about the 'lymphatic system'. You might not have heard of it, but it's very lucky that you have one. It consists of lymph nodes connected to a whole range of little tubes which are similar to veins. These 'lymphatic capillaries' don't carry blood though; they carry a clear watery substance called 'lymph'. This lymph drags impurities and dead stuff out of your system and keeps your body nice.

But thanks to Pandora, there has to be a kind of infection that targets even this little-known system. This disease is one of the worst that any nightmare can imagine, and if somebody made it up and put it in a book you probably wouldn't believe it. Once again mosquitoes carry the parasite around. In this case they are tiny little wiggling worms which are too small to be seen with the naked eye. They are called filariae and their larvae are called microfilariae. They are carried by the mosquito, and when the mosquito lands on some poor person the larvae are left on the skin where they burrow into the unsuspecting victim.

These microfilariae then carry out their evil plan. They migrate through skin, flesh and blood until they reach the lymphatic system.

Once there, they begin doing what all of these parasites love doing best – breeding. Soon millions and trillions of little wriggly worms are living in the lymph nodes and the whole system begins to shut down so that fluids can't be passed out of the legs and arms. This leads to hugely swollen arms, legs, feet and ankles that wouldn't look too bad on an elephant (in some cases it affects testicles which become basketball sized – Yowzer!!!).

But wait, there's more. Some filariae decide to live just under the skin of their poor host. They carry on and breed to such an extent that the skin begins to thicken, dry out, become flaky and turn grey – just like an elephant's.

I'm sure you'll agree that elephantiasis is a horrible disease. But filariasis cause even worse complaints. In one illness, called Onchocerciasis, the horrible critters set up shop in the host's eyeballs or else just under the skin where they become terribly, terribly itchy. At least that disease is not carried by a mosquito but a biting brown fly.

Lymphatic filariasis has been around for a very long time. The King of Punt visited the Egyptian Queen Hatshepsut (1501–1480 BC) and artists showed that his wife was infected with the disease. In Ancient Japan a medical picture showed a poor man carrying his enlarged testicles in a sling supported by a pole!

The Egyptians depicted Queen Ati with a wealthy/healthy figure.

BLOODSUCKERS AND MALARIA *135*

FACINATING FACT
THE BLOODSUCKERS HAVE IT

In the 18th Century there were all manner of funny sounding illnesses. Most doctors would look at the poor patient and command 'leech him'.

Whether they suffered from ablepsy, ague, anasarca, aphonia, aptha, apoplexy, atrophy, bilious fever, black death, black pox, brain fever, Bright's disease, bule, boils, cachexy, cacospysy, caduceus, canker, catalepsy, catarrhal, chioblain, chin cough, chlorosis, cholelithiasis, chorea, colic, consumption, congestive fever, costiveness, cramp colic, croup, cyanosis, cystities, day fever, debility, decrepitude, delirium tremens, deplumaiton, dairy fever, distemper, dock fever, dropsy, dry bellyache, dyscrasy, dysentry, dysorexy, dyspepsia, eclampsy, ecstasy, nephrosis, edema, eel thing, encephalitis, interocolitis, enteritis, epitaxis, erysipelas, falling sickness, fits, flux, French pox, great pox, grippe, grocer's itch, kings evil, hematuria, hemiplegy, hematemesis, horrors, hydrothorax, impetigo, inanition, lagrippe, lockjaw, lumbago, mania, marasmus, metritis, milk leg, mormal, morphew, mortification, necrosis, nepritis, nervous prostration, neuralagia, palsy, paroxysm, pemphigus, peritonitis, petechial fever, puerperal fever, phthisis, pleurisy, podarga, puerperal exhaustion, puking fever, putrid fever, rheumatism, rickets, sanguineous crust, roseola, sciatica, scirrhus, scotomoy, scrivener's palsy, screws, scrofula, scrumpox, shaking, shingles, siriasis, sloes, softening of the brain, spams, spotted fever, sprue, St. Vitas dance, strangery, swamp sickness, tick fever, trench mouth, variole, venesection, winter fever, or quinsy, the patients would have a course of leeches applied to their skin which would suck the poor patient's blood. (Actually one of the above complaints means the patient is dead. The leech would not be able to suck any blood. Can you guess which one?)

Doctors used these bloodsuckers so often that they were actually known as 'leeches'. It was big business and any doctor worth his salt carried a jar of them around ready to rent them out for a fee. In fact, even if patients went for a check-up, they were given a course of leeches as a type of spring cleaning.

We now know that bloodletting is one of the worst things you can do for a sick person. It means that their body can become dehydrated. When you are dehydrated it is much harder for blood to move oxygen around. Replacing lost blood cells takes a lot of energy and bleeding often made the sickness worse.

The most popular leech was the Hirudo medicinalis. This was one and half inches long before feeding but could grow out to as long as six inches to become a blood filled leech sausage! They have twenty stomachs and a sucker on both ends.

It usually took 15 minutes for them to fill up and drop off. When a surgeon wanted to make sure lots of blood was taken they would snip off the rear end of the leech. This meant the poor old leech became a never ending blood pump.

All in a day's work.

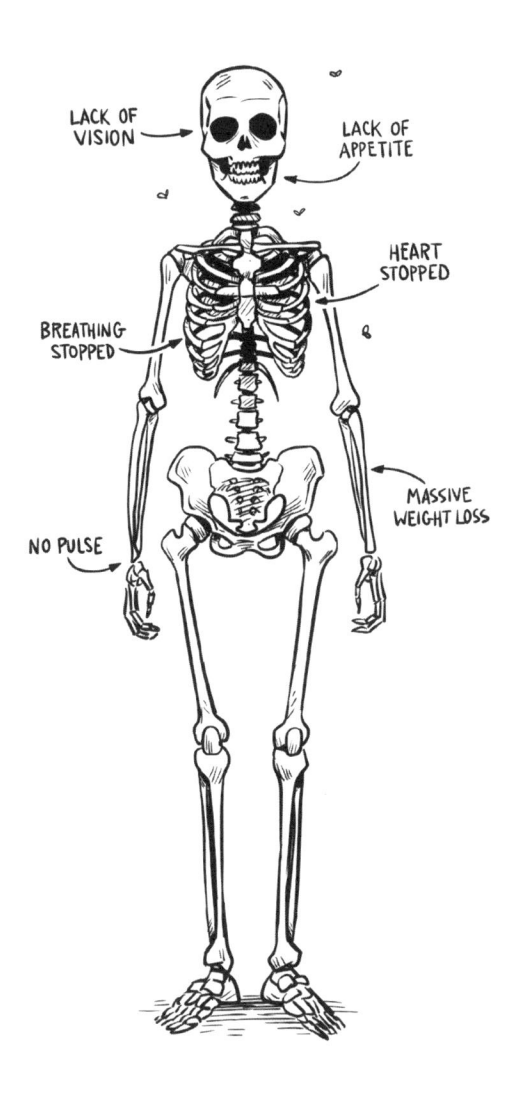

CHAPTER 10

DEATH
The end (?)

> **NAME:** Death, Deceased, Exctinct, Terminated
> **TRANSMISSION:** Lots of things
> **SYMPTOMS:** No pulse, breathing stopped, fly food
> **CURES:** None found yet
> **PROGNOSIS:** Not too good (unless you believe in reincarnation)

All our bodies go through several natural processes. Once the heart stops pumping blood around the body, cells are deprived of oxygen and begin to die. The blood pools at the lowest part of the body while the top part of the body goes pale and looks like grey wax. This is **THE FIRST STAGE OF DEATH** known as **PALLOR MORTIS**. Without a circulatory system to keep the body warm it begins to cool down. This is the **SECOND STAGE OF DEATH** known as **ALGOR MORTIS**.

Then, beginning in the eyelids neck and jaw, comes the **THIRD AND MOST FAMOUS STAGE OF DEATH** – you guessed it, **RIGOR MORTIS**. After about five hours the whole body goes as stiff as an ironing board and is almost impossible to move. (There is also a condition known as Extreme Rigor Mortis where the body is preserved with facial expression that the person died in, this is reserved for people who had particularly scary and horrible deaths, so is pretty horrible.)

This lasts for about twelve hours before **LIVOR MORTIS** sets in, where bits of the body begin to turn black and blue. While this is going on the body begins the process of **DECOMPOSITION**, when all those friendly little bacteria in your gut (which many take tablets or funny little drinks with weird Nordic names for) begin to break down your intestines. With none of the body's defenses to keep them in check some previously unimportant bacteria called clostridia and coliforms go into overdrive and spread through the stomach, the thighs and across the chest.

By this time the poor dead person is right into the **NEXT STAGE OF DEATH** called **PUTREFACATION**, which is all pretty darn horrible and it's best if you look away right now. Horrible smelly gasses begin to build up in the belly and guts, sometimes being squeezed out with farting or sighing sounds. Then the intestines are forced out of the rectum, the tongue is pushed out of the mouth and horribly, smelly fluids ooze out of the mouth and nostrils. At the same time flies have usually laid their eggs in the body and maggots are chowing down like gross wiggly white worms.

After too much of this kind of stuff to talk about any more, I'm relieved to say the **FINAL STAGE OF DEATH OCCURS – SKELETONISATION**.

All pretty horrible and it was lucky that the person was dead so that they didn't experience it.

The process of decomposition is a messy smelly business.

DID YOU KNOW
BACK FROM THE DEAD

There are a lot of bad horror movies around and you may have had the misfortune to watch one where a character who is dying sees their life flash before their eyes. These scenes invariably start with the person getting a kiss from mom before progressing to the first day at school, graduation, first love, marriage, kids, winning the Super Bowl etc etc. Well it seems that this is a real experience suffered by many as they die. The condition has the scientific name of LRE – Life Review Experience.

Scientists have interviewed hundreds of people who have had Near Death Experiences. Their hearts have stopped beating, and as their body shut down many saw key events in their life in a vivid way, almost like having your own smartphone in your head. When they underwent emergency CPR they were revived and reported what they had seen.

The main difference with the movies is that, and this is the freaky part, the memories weren't in order, but came higgledy piggledy into the person's consciousness and sometimes two or three played at once, all the while recreating the emotions felt when it happened. Many told of a sense of timelessness, they may have only been clinically dead for one or two minutes but felt they had been away for hundreds of years, or a moment. Go figure.

Memories are stored in different parts of the brain such as the prefrontal cortices and it is possible that they go into overdrive when other parts of the brain are shutting down. Or maybe it's proof that there is life after death. What do you think?

DEAD BODIES

Everybody knows about how the Ancient Egyptians preserved bodies but this is not a boring school book so we're going to go straight to the Victorians and see how they preserved the dead.

POST MORTEM PHOTOGRAPHY

The Victorian English were keen to prove that they were followers of fashion. One must-have for every good Victorian, was a photo on their mantelpiece showing a picture of 'Dear Old Departed Uncle George'. What's wrong with that you may ask. I meant to write 'Dear Old DEPARTED AND DEAD Uncle George'. It wasn't good enough to have a picture of him alive, to really show your love you had to have photos of them when they were dead!

Uncle George was the life of the party.

Once a relative passed this 'mortal coil' (earthly life) the local photographer would be summoned. Not only did he unload his big old Brown Bess Camera and tripod, he would also unload his 'Dead Relative Posing Apparatus' (I'm not sure that's what they called it, but I can't find its real name). Hopefully the photographer didn't live too far away or the weather was not too hot because that meant the 'Dearly Departed' was becoming 'Shockingly Smelly'.

Photographers became skilled at posing the dead to make them look lifelike, using props and makeup. They were often posed with living family members to recreate what they looked like in life. How the rest of the family managed to stay still for the 30 seconds or so required to expose the negative, and not run screaming from the room, is beyond me. The saddest Victorian death photos are those that show entire families or sets of siblings laid low by an outbreak of disease. This practice of immortalizing the dead was known as memento more or memorial portraiture.

The best photographers had loads of props and gadgets to make the body look as lifelike as possible. Frames could stand up and pose the corpse, while some practitioners painted life-like eyes on the corpse's closed eyelids. Young women were often dressed in wedding gowns to show what they would have looked like had they lived to see their own wedding day. Children were shown with living siblings or with parents, or with favorite objects such as dolls or pets. Children were often photographed as if peacefully sleeping, but the ravages of disease are often present in the hollow cheeks and sunken eyes of the dead belying any attempt to make the poor poppets lifelike. Sometimes make-up was applied, or the photographic image tinted to give them rosy cheeks.

The group shots were popular, this was done because photography was new, but still quite rare and expensive, and it might be the only photograph the family would ever have of the loved one. Since the photographer was there and everyone was already bathed and dressed up, why not get the whole family together? Many were posed leaning on their siblings' shoulders or sitting up in the warm embrace of their doting parents. The fact that the photographer was able to arrange the cadaver in a lifelike pose indicates that the session was at least 36 hours after death. As you'll remember, 6 to 8 hours after death rigor-mortis sets in, 24 to 84 hours afterwards the body becomes flaccid. A dead mother holding her dead baby in her lap could be arranged as if giving a loving embrace, but it is impossible to get the dead hand to grasp the loved ones' limbs. Eyes of the dead could not focus on an object, leaving the loved cadaver to gaze silently into space. The idea of spending an hour with a dead loved one being manipulated and posed surrounded by children and parents may seem pretty darn horrible to us, but the Victorians were surrounded by death.

Death was ever present, loved ones would be laid out in the parlor for up to a week, and family and friends could be struck down unexpectedly without rhyme or reason. Often the body would have emitted quite a stench, but such was the bond between members of a family that the love they held for their deceased relative shines through in all of these photos.

"Say cheese!"

OTHER EMBALMING TECHNIQUES

Just as meat needed to be preserved for a rainy day in medieval Europe, so too did they learn how to embalm corpses. The methods were fairly primitive and often involved removing the internal organs and stuffing the body with herbs to minimize putrefaction.

Death was often turned into a political statement. Members of the Habsburg dynasty of Austria who had the misfortune to die would not be buried as a full corpse, bits and pieces would be chopped off the cadaver and sent to all corners of the empire. For a long time, it was the custom to bury the body, the heart and the intestines separately. The body would be buried in a church somewhere within the empire, the

DEATH *145*

heart would be buried somewhere else that needed a token of Imperial appreciation, while the intestines and bowels would be buried in the vaults of the holiest of holies in Vienna, St Stephens. Go figure.

The crusades saw a need for European nobility to improve preservation techniques as many fallen knights and lords wanted to be buried on their estates. Bodies were often boiled before being packed into barrels and preserved in salt or fats.

One uniquely preserved medieval corpse was St Bees man, found in 1981 in the ruin of a Chancel in the church of the same name. Whether it was intended by his nearest and dearest that he should be well preserved is open to question but a unique set of circumstances ensured that his corpse was just like new. He is the most complete body of a medieval nobleman ever discovered. Two sets of burials were investigated in the archaeological dig. One set was composed of the monks who lived in the St Bees priory and the other assemblage was made up of people living between about 1120 CE and 1300 CE. Within a well-constructed vault was a wooden coffin. Within the wooden coffin was a lead coffin which was sealed with a layer of clay. When the lead coffin was opened it revealed a figure wrapped in several waxy burial shrouds. When the shrouds were removed a remarkably well preserved body was revealed, so well preserved that he seemed to peer out from his hooded lids at the excavating team.

The skin had a fresh pink appearance which faded quickly. The eyes were in good condition and the mouth was not desiccated. Internal tissues were well preserved and, when the autopsy was being performed, it was possible to see blood that was still a dark red viscous fluid. The internal organs were well preserved and when the liver was cut open it was red, although it quickly faded to brown.

The top of the coffin, also lead, had been soldered-down to form an airtight seal. The lead coffin was originally encased with wood, but this had rotted away, leaving only rusty marks of the iron bindings.

In later times different navies had different ways of preserving their dead. Spanish and Portuguese ships used rocks for their ballast that had been blessed by a priest, making it consecrated ground. Deceased mariners were packed into this soil and, should the ship be fortunate enough to reach home, the deceased sailor was extracted from his shipborne cemetery and re-interned in a proper cemetery on his home soil. Admiral Nelson was preserved by folding his body into a barrel of brandy where it became pickled on the way home. Lesser sailors in the British navy were not so fortunate. They were wrapped in a shroud of old sailcloth with a round shot bound to the feet. The sailcloth was firmly sewed up by a ship mate whose final stitch went through the nose of the deceased, just to make sure that he was dead. They were then tipped overboard to plummet down into the icy depths.

A lucky escape.

IN THE MODERN FUNERAL PARLOUR

The funeral business is big business – just remember there are three certainties in life: death, taxes, and boy bands.

Once a body gets to a funeral parlour there are certain things undertakers do to prepare the body for viewing. Firstly, they have to glue the eyes and lips together. The skin of a corpse dries out and this makes the eyes and lips draw back revealing skull like teeth and sunken eyes, not a nice sight for the guests. There's a myth that hair and finger nails keep growing after death but this is just because the skin draws back, making the hair and nails more prominent.

Undertakers often ask for a photo of the dead person so that they can apply makeup that makes the subject look as lifelike as possible. You might have seen pictures of people in coffins with their heads raised on pillows. This is not to make it look like the person is having a nice nap, its so the blood doesn't pool around the face making horrible big black and blue blotches. They also use embalming fluids to slow down the process of decomposition. A good mortician will concentrate on the face and the hands and modern day embalming fluids kill bacteria as well as repelling insects! (Fascinating Fact!!!)

Once the body is buried in its coffin it can take many years for the body to decompose and skeletonize. A body that is not buried decomposes twice as fast as one submerged in water and eight times faster than one buried in dry earth. This is known in grave digging circles as 'Casper's Law.'

DID YOU KNOW
CREMATION FACT FILE

When Christianity became popular in Western Europe cremation became unpopular because it was thought that a cremated person could not be resurrected.

Cremation became popular in the 19th Century when big cities ran out of burial space.

An average man's remains will weigh approximately 7.4 pounds after cremation while a woman will be reduced to about 5.8 pounds.

Modern day crematoria get to temperatures of 870–980 °C (1,600–1,800 °F).

The heat burns the body, unlike in James Bond movies, the flames never touch the corpse.

After cremation all that is left is bone fragments called cremains. These are then ground down by a special machine to make 'the ashes'. It wouldn't be nice to see Great Aunty Doris' teeth poking out of the ashes.

Some 'cremains' can contain a nasty surprise.

Fake breasts are removed before cremation as otherwise the cremains stick to them making 'ash-boobs'. (Not a technical term.) Many poisoners try to get their victims cremated straight away so that an autopsy can't reveal poisons such as arsenic. Arsenic stays in a dead body for up to ten years.

Pacemakers are removed before cremation, otherwise they explode!

The earliest known cremation is of Mungo Lady, an Australian cremation dated to about 20,000 BCE.

Artificial metal knees and hips are removed before cremations and sold second hand!!! (I'm not sure this is a fact but it sounds good.)

"Thank you for your attention. See you again in Book 2 – If you're lucky."

Glossary of terms

Analgesic – A drug that controls pain such as aspirin or codeine.

Apothecary – A person who prepared and sold medicines and drugs.

BCE – Before Common Era – any year before 1 CE.

Castration – The surgical removal of testicles.

Cauterised – Where a wound is burnt with a hot iron or gunpowder to seal it and stop bleeding.

CE – Common Era – any year after year 1.

Circulatory System – System of arteries and veins that carry blood around the body as it is pumped by the heart. The blood carries oxygen from the lungs into all of the organs and cells.

Cysts – Small growths filled with liquid or foreign tissue.

Digestive System – beginning with the mouth and ending with the bum. Food passes down the throat, into the stomach and then into the large and small intestines. On the way nutrients are extracted and wastes are excreted.

Endemic – A disease or condition regularly found in a particular area.

Epidemic – A widespread outbreak of an infection or unpleasant thing. Walking while texting and swearing are good non-medical examples.

Hominid – A primate of a family (Hominidae) which includes humans and their fossil ancestors.

Host – A biological entity that has a parasite living within it or on it. (Can also refer to human politicians and lawyers.)

Incontinence – An inability to control when the body does number ones and twos.

Immune – When an individual cannot get sick from a certain disease.

Immunisation – The process of making a person or animal immune to infection, typically by inoculation.

Mortality Rate – % of people who will die once they get sick.

Necrotic – Dead, usually a bit smelly.

Ones and Twos – A polite way of saying wee and poo. Cockney third = turd.

Protozoa – A group of tiny single celled animals which include amoebas, flagellates and sporozoans.

151

J. J. 'Malodorous' Moore has been a writer for longer than he can remember. He's spent a lifetime reading about the weird, the fascinating and the downright gruesome. Specialising in 'out there' material, Jonathan J. Moore promises that whenever you read his books your eyes will be opened to a whole lot of new stuff.

K. B. 'Barnstormer' Moon is a self-taught artist who with her deft hand loves to draw the irksome and icky. Kate has worked as an animator, character artist and illustrator on all sorts of film and print projects.

First published in 2018 by New Holland Publishers
London • Sydney • Auckland

131-151 Great Titchfield Street, London WIW 5BB, United Kingdom
1/66 Gibbes Street, Chatswood, NSW 2067, Australia
5/39 Woodside Ave, Northcote, Auckland 0627, New Zealand

newhollandpublishers.com

Copyright © 2018 New Holland Publishers
Copyright © 2018 in text: Jonathan J. Moore
Copyright © 2018 in images: Kate B. Moon

All rights reserved. No part of this publication may be reproduced, stored in a retrieval system or transmitted, in any form or by any means, electronic, mechanical, photocopying, recording or otherwise, without the prior written permission of the publishers and copyright holders.

A record of this book is held at the British Library and the National Library of Australia.

ISBN 9781921024962

Group Managing Director: Fiona Schultz
Publisher: Alan Whiticker
Project Editor: Kaitlyn Smith
Designer: Sara Lindberg
Production Director: James Mills-Hicks
Book Reviewer: Samuel Capell
Printer: Toppan Leefung Printing Limited

10 9 8 7 6 5 4 3 2 1

Keep up with New Holland Publishers on Facebook
facebook.com/NewHollandPublishers

UK £6.99
US $14.99